NEW MEXICO

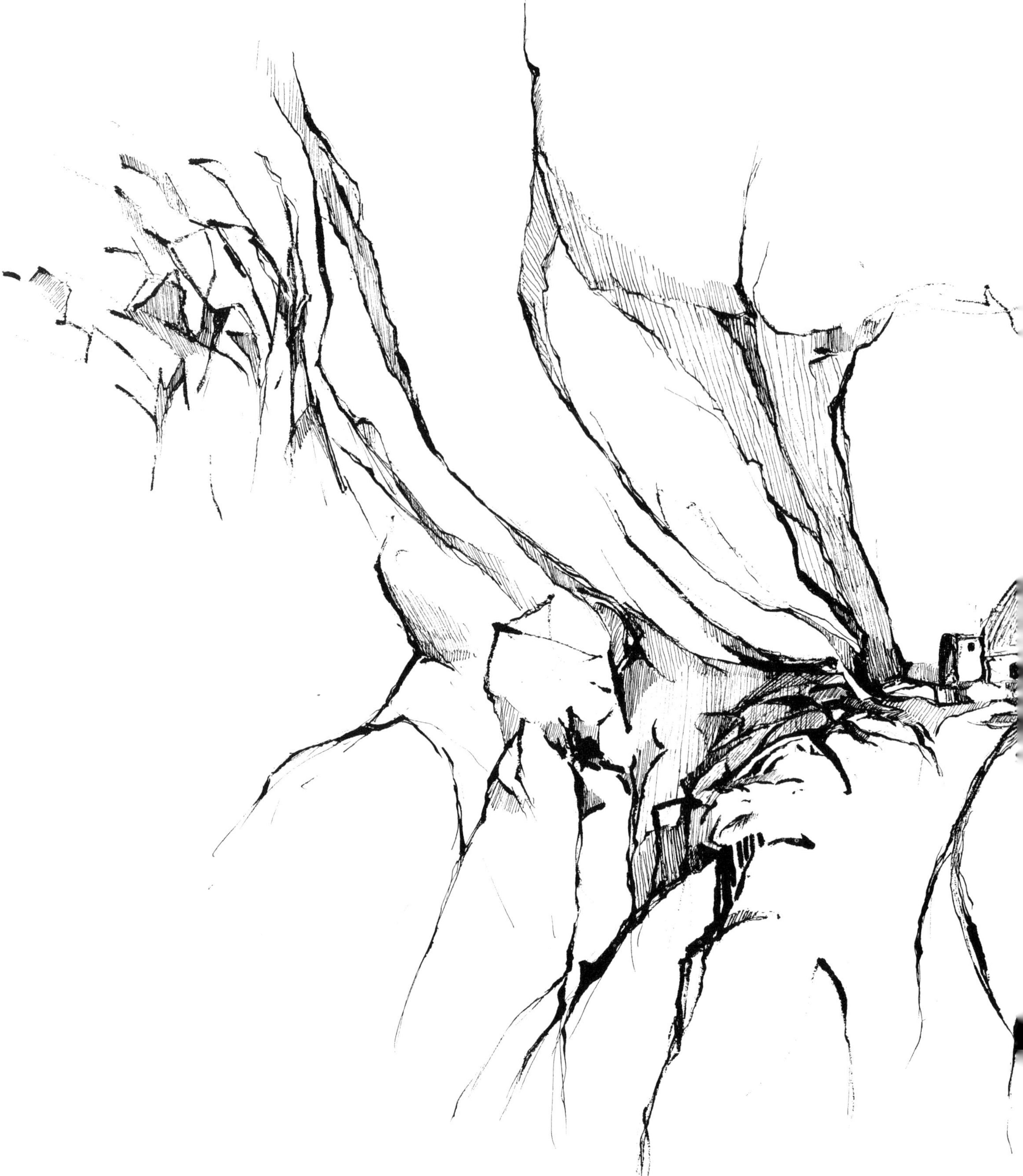

NEW MEXICO
Gift of the Earth

RUSSELL D. BUTCHER

Foreword by
George H. Ewing

A STUDIO BOOK
THE VIKING PRESS · NEW YORK

*To my wife, Pam,
who loves the enchanted land
as much as I do*

Pen-and-ink sketches by Polly Schaafsma

Drawings of Pueblo Indian pottery motifs by the author

Text and black-and-white illustrations Copyright © 1975
by Russell D. Butcher
Color illustrations Copyright 1975 in all countries of the
International Copyright Union by Russell D. Butcher
All rights reserved
First published in 1975 by The Viking Press, Inc.
625 Madison Avenue, New York, N.Y. 10022
Published simultaneously in Canada by
The Macmillan Company of Canada Limited
SBN 670-50758-x
Library of Congress catalog card number: 75-533
Text and black-and-white illustrations printed in U.S.A.
Color illustrations printed in Japan

Acknowledgments

I am lovingly grateful to my wife, Pam, for her hours of slaving over the typewriter, pushing out the manuscript, and for her invaluable encouragement and editorial suggestions.

I deeply appreciate the many kindnesses and help of Alden C. and Gretchen Hayes, James F. and Sally Richards, Drs. Walter R. and Sally Spofford, Monica Warner Fager, and also Polly Schaafsma, for her contribution to this book.

A special word of thanks is also due to Frank F. Kowski, former Director of the National Park Service's Southwest Regional Office in Santa Fe; and Linwood E. Jackson, Superintendent of Bandelier National Monument.

Also by Russell D. Butcher **MAINE PARADISE**

My friend was wrong who said that this country was so old it does not matter what we . . . do here. What we do anywhere matters, but especially here. It matters very much.
—Edith Warner in
The House at Otowi Bridge

Contents

	Foreword by George H. Ewing	9
	Preface	11
I	Exploring Through Time	13
II	Looking to the Future	113
	Map	118
	Notes to the Plates	119
	Notes to the Drawings	122
	Chronology	123
	Some Further Reading	126

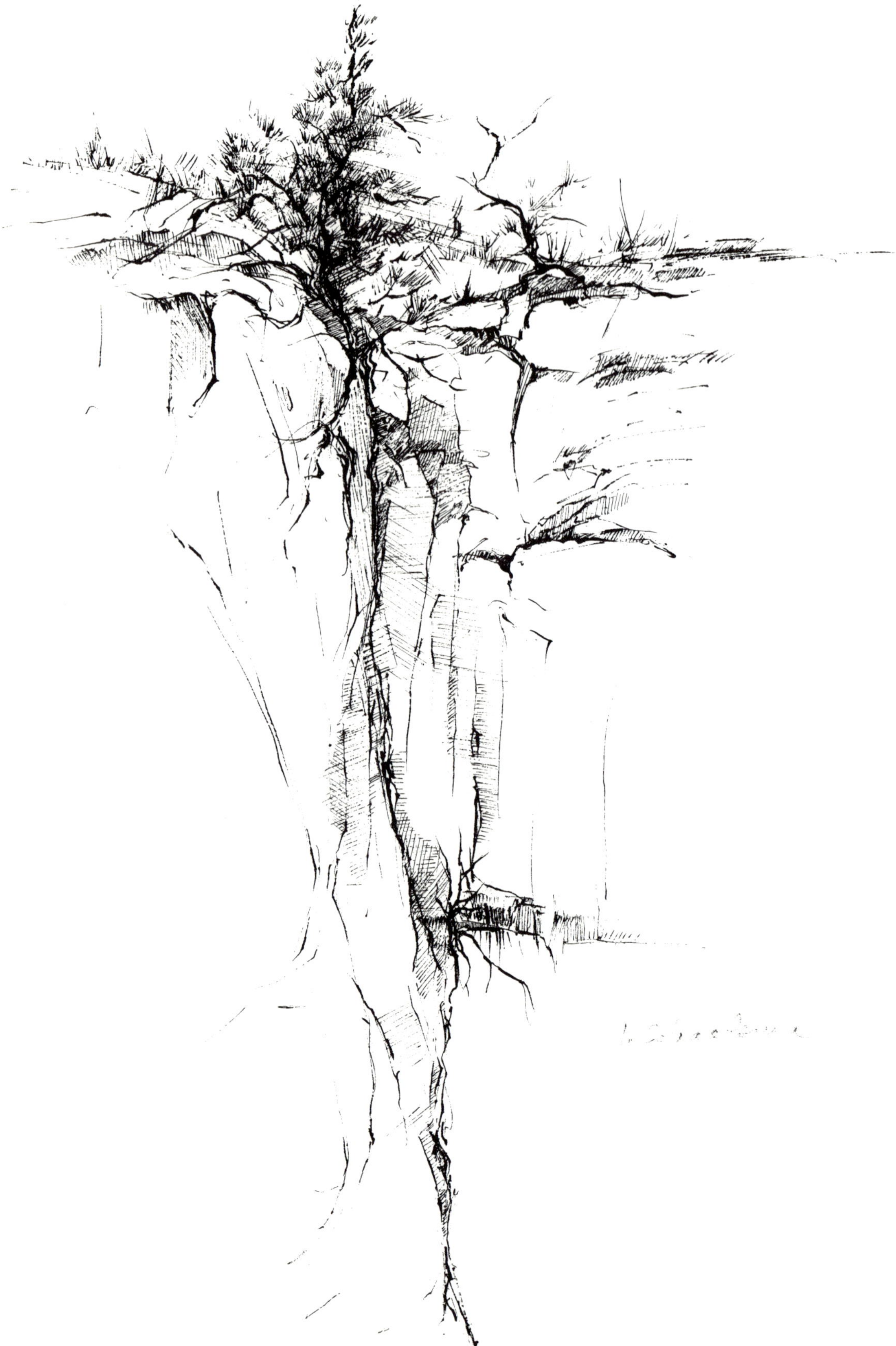

Foreword

To many, the name New Mexico conjures up a vision of a desert and nothing else. I hope that this book will serve to dispel that image. There is desert in New Mexico, to be sure, but there is much else. It is not a serene and placid land, however; it is a land which challenges the senses with bright skies and horizon-sweeping vistas; it stretches the imagination, too, into wonder at what lies beyond the horizon and what lies back in the past.

Those who come to New Mexico for the first time should come with minds open and free of preconception. Adventure and excitement and rare beauty await those who seek it here, whether it be in the discovery of desert plants in bloom or the wonder of a deep, spired limestone cavern, or the timeless solitude of an ancient Indian ruin. In New Mexico, too, there comes an almost overwhelming sense of being a part of nature, for the features of this land bespeak the magnitude of the forces which lie beneath this earth and on it. There are rugged, towering mountain ranges and deep-cut canyons, wind-sculptured sandstone cliffs and tumbled lava masses, and everywhere the mark of endless time. In such surroundings one's self and being assume a different proportion.

For all this, the land of New Mexico has been tolerant of humankind, has accepted us and borne our works with dignity. To the Indian people who came here millennia ago it gave sustenance, and substance for their dwellings. The hardy Spanish colonists who pressed northward out of Mexico in the seventeenth century found a lifeway adapted to and partly dictated by the land, and even the forces of change of the nineteenth and twentieth centuries and the people who came carrying the tools and technology of that change have made adjustment here. Unlike so many regions, this one has seen its past not destroyed but carried on into the present. Thus one may find here a variety of peoples and hear a mixture of languages and see ancient Pueblo villages and centers of advanced scientific research.

But there is danger here for the newcomer; once seen, the land is difficult to leave and more difficult to forget. Russ Butcher has never really left, nor has he forgotten. Let him lead you into and through New Mexico, whether or not circumstances permit you to come in person. You are in able hands, and you will see through sensitive eyes. But heed his concern for the future. We have too few areas left in this country where the past lives on and the spirit can partake of nature undespoiled. Help us use this ancient and beautiful land well and wisely for our benefit and yours.

George H. Ewing
Director
Museum of New Mexico, Santa Fe

Preface

The first autumn we moved to Santa Fe followed an especially hot, muggy summer in New England. Returning to the high, dry air and brilliant sunshine of the Southwest was like being liberated. I had been there before, but only to visit.

For the first few months we (my wife, Pam, and I) lived in a tiny adobe compound—complete with pine *vigas,* a corner fireplace in the bathroom, Mexican tilework in the kitchen, and a small private patio out front.

The adobe city was full of flavor. The bright colors of Lombardy poplars and cottonwoods spread their gold above houses that blended with the earth, deep vibrant yellow chamiso grew against adobe walls, and purple asters lined the roadsides. As cool evenings came on, the fragrance of juniper smoke drifted from a thousand fireplaces—a sweet aroma that stays with you, hauntingly.

I was very fortunate that year to have landed a public relations position with the Museum of New Mexico, and, in my work, to begin to gain a better understanding of the state's unique tri-culture in archaeology, history, and the arts.

On weekends and holidays we ventured forth in all directions, into high meadows and aspen groves of the Sangre de Cristos, along the Rio Grande to Velarde where apples, peaches, and long strings of bright red chili peppers were for sale, and through foothills to Hispanic mountain villages to see weavers and woodcarvers at work. We made pilgrimages to Indian pueblos to watch ceremonial dances, followed the river to see great flocks of migratory waterfowl, and came back again to explore more prehistoric ruins.

Later we lived on a pinyon pine-and-juniper-covered hilltop overlooking Tesuque Valley, just north of Santa Fe. Within our view were a chicken ranch, fruit orchards, and a tiny adobe church across the way. The Sangre de Cristos rose five thousand feet above us, their summits above timberline turning a blaze of orange and pink at sunset.

Winters in New Mexico are just magic—the air is crisp and invigorating, and there is a brilliant blue sky nearly every day. Our first Christmas in Santa Fe was bitterly cold and snowy, but the warm glow of *luminarias* decoratively outlined the roofs and walls of homes and downtown buildings.

Spring is the time of strong winds and blowing sand. But it also brings the purple lilacs and fruit trees into bloom. Summer is dry heat, violent thunderstorms, and flash floods sweeping down the arroyos. It is also the time of pink and red hollyhocks and brilliant magenta blossoms of the cane cholla cactus . . . and the time for tourists.

The more we have come to know New Mexico, the more this enchanted land has seemed a world apart. So much of what man has done over the centuries to live here reflects the land itself, its colors and forms across the vast distances, its very substance. There is a feeling that the people who live here haven't yet lost a sense of the fundamentals that make life meaningful.

The text that follows consists of brief vignettes about New Mexico, presented roughly within the sequence of the state's long human history. There is, of course, so much more one could say about each place, and of many others left unmentioned. Nevertheless, I hope that this book will increase the reader's appreciation and enjoyment of this beautiful, ancient land.

R.D.B.

Looking toward the Peloncillo Mountains
May 1974

I

Exploring Through Time

Driving south through the Front Range cities of Colorado and climbing over Raton Pass into New Mexico, one drops onto a vast grassland that turns golden in autumn, with roadsides brightened by mile after mile of tall yellow sunflowers, against dark mountains in the distance.

A few miles east of Raton, in the midst of the high plains dotted here and there with volcanic cinder cones such as Capulin Mountain, is a place where archaeologists have discovered evidence of some of man's earliest activity in the Southwest—dating back eleven thousand to twelve thousand years. Those early hunters, called Folsom man, once ranged from Mexico to Alaska, living on wild animals. At this particular site a well-shaped spearpoint was found buried with the bones of a species of large bison that has been extinct for thousands of years.

Even earlier evidence of man has been discovered elsewhere in New Mexico, including at a site on the plains near Clovis and in a Sandia Mountains cave near Albuquerque. In the latter careful digging revealed crudely flaked spearpoints, dating back to the far wetter climate of at least fifteen thousand years ago, with the bones of such long-extinct native animals as the mammoth, mastodon, camel, and horse.

Southwest of Raton the highway crosses the grasslands toward the great Sangre de Cristo Mountains, and then follows the Cimarron River upstream. Soon after entering a canyon, the road passes a stretch of spectacular sheer cliffs known as the Cimarron Palisades. We were there one autumn as the cottonwood trees along the rushing stream were beginning to turn gold. In the late afternoon the rich sunlight highlighted the eight-hundred-foot-high columnar formations of yellowish rock. A little gray dipper flew from rock to rock, bobbing comically, and now and then dashed right into the swiftly flowing current in search of food.

Continuing over the mountains to Taos, one is suddenly struck by the imposing grandeur of the Sangre de Cristos as they rise abruptly from the flat sagebrush plains. Taos itself is a charming old town—dusty and full of character. Back in the 1890s it began to draw artists from all over the world who came to portray the mountains, valleys, Hispanic mountain villages, and the Pueblo Indian dances of the surrounding region. It is still one of New Mexico's largest art centers; its streets are lined with art galleries, a scattering of museums, bookstores, and restaurants varied enough to satisfy almost any taste—from the hot peppery Mexican food to organic dishes. Most of the homes and commercial buildings are of unadorned brown adobe that blends with the earth.

Nearby is the Pueblo of Taos, the only modern Indian village that is terraced upward, four and five stories high, much like some of the larger pueblos of prehistoric New Mexico. Between the two blocks of dwellings there is a large dance plaza where religious ceremonies are publicly performed. Through this plaza flows a clear stream whose waters originate at Blue Lake, high in the Sangre de Cristos. The small fir-bordered lake is sacred to the people of Taos Pueblo, for to them its waters represent the source and sustenance of life. A few years ago, after nationwide public support developed for the pueblo people, Congress finally removed supervision of Blue Lake, with some forty-eight thousand acres of surrounding forested watershed, from Carson National Forest, and returned it to the pueblo in recognition of its deeply religious significance to the Indians.

After passing across flat barren country in the arid, almost treeless northwest corner of the state for so many miles that one begins to despair of ever reaching the destination, the dirt road finally crosses the boundary of Chaco Canyon National Monument, swings down a narrow rocky draw, and emerges onto the expanse of the canyon itself.

Chaco is a wild and desolate place. Low, buff-colored cliffs rise only fifty to a hundred feet. The canyon floor is spacious, averaging perhaps a mile or so across, and its flat bottom is covered with low-growing desert plants such as saltbush, greasewood, and sagebrush. A winding arroyo, normally dry except after torrential summer thunderstorms, has cut a deep incision down the middle of the canyon floor. Here and there along its course grow a few deeply rooted cottonwoods, willows, and tamarisks.

The canyon's real source of fame, however, is the fantastic ruins of the once great towns of the Anasazi, "the ancient ones," who lived eight hundred to nine hundred years ago. Both their size and quality of construction make them the finest array of prehistoric pueblo ruins in North America.

There are ten major town sites along a nine-mile stretch of Chaco, and others beyond. Most of them lie along the north side of the canyon, close to the massive cliffs, while several are perched atop the canyon rims above. They have such names as Wijiji, Hungo Pavie, Chettro Kettle, Pueblo Bonito, Pueblo del Arroyo, Kin Kletso, Casa Chiquita, and Peñasco Blanco. Many of them have never, or only barely, been investigated by archaeologists. Others, such as the large rectangular Chettro Kettle, have been partly excavated. Chettro Kettle is built around an open dance plaza, in the middle of which is a great subterranean kiva—a room that was used in conjunction with the community's religious observances.

Only Pueblo Bonito has been completely excavated and stabilized. The National Park Service provides a self-guiding tour of this great D-shaped ruin. Bonito spreads over about three acres of ground, and at its height of development is believed to have contained about eight hundred rooms reaching to four and five stories high around the rear curved wall, accommodating an estimated twelve hundred people.

Some of the ruins in this maze of small rooms still have their ceilings perfectly intact. The log *vigas* which the Anasazi cut with their stone axes from distant ponderosa pine forests hundreds of years ago have been preserved through time by the dry climate. Crosswise to these supporting beams, the Indians placed smaller *latias* of peeled willow sprouts, and on top of them were laid strips of split juniper and bark, covered finally by a few inches of packed earth to form the floor of the room above.

The massive masonry walls of Bonito are in themselves a work of art, for they are carefully faced with alternating bands of large stone blocks and narrow layers of thin stonework. During one of our visits there we walked across the two dance plazas and around the many sunken kivas, just as the setting sun was flooding the walls around us with an orange glow, making a pattern of light and shade that accentuated the patterns of masonry.

As we have explored Bonito and looked down on it from the canyon rim behind, we have wondered, with the archaeologists, why, after so many centuries of living in pithouses and then in small clusters of dwellings, some of the Chaco residents of about A.D. 1030 suddenly began building these large, terraced, apartment-house-like towns. What motivated them to desire more communal living? As yet there are no clear answers; but it is evident that their new, more interdependent lifestyle contributed toward more highly developed arts and crafts, as well as a new architecture. For they made beautifully decorated pottery, which they formed from coils of clay and without the benefit of a wheel, just as the modern Pueblo Indians do today. Black-on-white Chaco bowls, pitchers, ladles, and bowl-and-handle dippers of distinctive shapes are decorated with black mineral paint in finely drawn hachuring patterns that zig-zag around the inside of bowls and the outside of pitchers; or there are interlocking scrolls, frets, triangles, and checkerboard-like designs.

Why then, by the late 1200s, were all the pueblos of Chaco Canyon abandoned, so soon after the flowering of civilization? Was it drought or changing climatic patterns, depleted soil, lowered water tables, or was it a combination of environmental factors that contributed to the collapse of the people's socio-religious organization? No one really knows; but it is believed fairly certain that many, if not most, Chacoans moved eastward to the Rio Grande Valley where water supplies during periods of drought were more reliable.

About fifty-five miles north of Chaco Canyon, on the banks of the Animas River, rises the ruin of another great Anasazi pueblo. Although its history is not connected with that of the people of central Mexico, it is called Aztec Ruins.

This pueblo was initially built from about A.D. 1110 to 1124, by people whose architectural and pottery techniques were essentially the same as those of Chaco Canyon. It was then abandoned for a period of years, but was reoccupied from about A.D. 1220 to 1260 by a second Anasazi group who apparently moved from Mesa Verde, some thirty miles to the northwest in southwestern Colorado. These newcomers were not satisfied with the specifications of the old pueblo, so they set about remodeling it by partitioning old rooms, making doorways smaller, and adding new rooms and kivas built of rounded cobblestones—copying what they had been accustomed to in the more cramped quarters of Mesa Verde's cave dwellings.

Another interesting feature of Aztec Ruins is the impressive, reconstructed Great Kiva. Although not quite as large as the solitary great kiva across Chaco Canyon from Pueblo Bonito, Casa Rinconada, which has a sixty-four-foot diameter, Aztec's restoration nevertheless gives the visitor an excellent idea of what the great ceremonial kivas were like. In the subdued light of this huge circular chamber, one can almost visualize the Indians performing sacred ceremonies to the beat of drums and chanting voices—the sound rising to the great timbered roof that rests upon four massive pillars.

The site of this ancient pueblo is protected within Aztec Ruins National Monument. Visitors may enjoy a self-guided walk through the area and a series of exhibits in the pueblo-style Visitor Center.

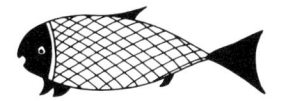

A million years ago in northern New Mexico, a huge mountain erupted, sending molten lava flows and tremendous clouds of volcanic ash down upon the surrounding land. Successive layers of lava and ash gradually created a plateau many hundreds of feet thick around the mountain's base. The huge eruption is believed to have been one of the largest anywhere, several times greater than Krakatau whose ash and smoke dimmed the sun around the world in 1883.

When finally the violence deep within the earth subsided, the mountain-top collapsed, forming one of the world's largest calderas, el Valle Grande. Once the huge crater was filled with water, as is Crater Lake in Oregon. Eventually the water drained away, and today the valley is a vast pine-and-spruce-bordered grassy bowl where cattle graze in summer. The surrounding remnants of the volcano are now the thickly forested peaks of the Jemez Mountains, where deer, elk, and other wildlife abound, and hikers follow trails into the remote wilderness.

The first time I drove through el Valle Grande only a narrow dirt track crossed the mountains, and winter's snow was just melting. For miles I slipped and sloshed through deep mud, hoping at every dip and turn that the car would not get bogged down. Finally as dusk was coming on, the road at long last began climbing out of the east side of the valley, heading into a forest of tall trees. Just as it seemed as though I had made it, there dead ahead of me, in the glare of the headlights, lay a gigantic log of a fallen pine completely blocking the way. Hours later I finally retraced my way to the paved highway in Jemez Canyon, vowing never to see Jemez crater again.

But we have returned, many times, now that the road is paved. Once we watched enchanted as showers of golden aspen leaves flickered down, covering the new snow of an early autumn storm, among stately pines and spruces whose boughs were weighted down in perfect symmetry.

During the ensuing hundreds of thousands of years after the volcanic eruption, streams slowly carved sheer-walled canyons into the layers of lava and ash of the Pajarito Plateau, at the eastern edge of the Jemez Mountains, eventually leaving long arms of flat-topped mesas between. Forests of pine and juniper covered the land, and for a long time nomadic people roamed through the region, hunting and gathering edible wild plants.

In the late 1200s and early 1300s, during a period of severe drought in the Southwest when many of the Anasazi are believed to have moved into the Rio Grande Valley, some of the pueblo people discovered the canyons and mesas of the Pajarito and decided to settle there. One such place is the secluded and beautiful little canyon of el Rito de los Frijoles, now within Bandelier National Monument.

Bandelier is one of our favorite places in New Mexico. Only an hour's drive from Santa Fe, and much less from Los Alamos, the Monument protects more than twenty-nine thousand acres of the plateau—most of it an unspoiled roadless wilderness.

From the pueblo-style Visitor Center buildings at the road's end, we have explored many parts of the Frijoles. Sometimes on a bright winter morning, following an overnight snowfall, we have hiked the trails as the warm sun quickly melted the sparkling mantle of snow. Sometimes in summer—as great cumulus clouds mushroomed over the mountains, deafening thunderbolts resounded in the canyon, and rain created a hundred waterfalls tumbling down the cliffs.

We have come to Bandelier in autumn when the leaves of the narrow-leaf cottonwoods had turned gold, and the hillsides and mesas were covered with clumps of purple asters and a variety of yellow flowers. We have often followed the trail up-canyon to the intimate, shaded narrows where big-leaf maples grow; and down-canyon through groves of tall pines, low clumps of Gambel oaks, and little grassy meadows—coming at length to two waterfalls that plunge from ledges of resistant lava rock and spray into clear pools below. Continuing on into the deepest part of the Frijoles, one comes upon the roiled rapids of the Rio Grande, within White Rock Canyon. At other times we have hiked for miles across the wilderness into deep gorges and other canyons.

A short walk from the Visitor Center leads to a wide meadow, in the middle of which sprawls the ruins of the almost circular pueblo, Tyuonyi. Only low walls of rounded rocks suggest the arrangement and size of what were once as many as four hundred small rooms terraced to three stories around a central plaza. The village also contained four kivas—three sunken into the plaza and a larger one close by.

From the pueblo ruins the trail climbs up the talus slope to the base of the one-hundred-fifty- to two-hundred-foot-high yellowish cliffs that form the spectacular north wall of the canyon. Along the base of the escarpment are more ruins of dwellings, where the Indians had discovered they could carve hollows and small rooms into the softly compacted volcanic ash, called tuff. In front of these hollows they built stone-and-mud houses, their flat roofs supported by *vigas*. Some of these cliff-base houses were terraced against the cliff, to two or three stories. One can still see lines of small holes in the rock above where the ends of *vigas* had been lodged. Nearby is a tiny cave kiva carved entirely out of the rock.

Groups of these dwellings extended for nearly two miles along the canyon, and archaeologists have reconstructed one of the building units to show what they were like. Typically, as in all prehistoric Southwest pueblos, the rooms were relatively small—measuring about six by nine feet across and five to six feet high, with doorways measuring three feet by half as wide. These were rather cramped quarters by our standards; but the inhabitants had no elaborate furnishings, and they spent nearly all their waking hours outdoors.

Certainly the people of Frijoles lived close to the land, in harmony with nature. The Pueblo Indians still consider themselves an integral part of the natural environment, observing seasonal cycles of religious ceremonies and other rituals that are believed essential for the sequences of nature to occur properly. The laws of the supernatural powers must be obeyed and properly appealed to, so that the pueblo community may experience harmony and the all-important blessings of rain and crop fertility.

The women of the pueblo made pottery, cooked the meals, wove baskets and sandals from the fibrous leaves of the yucca, made coarsely woven cotton cloth, prepared animal skins for winter clothing, and ground corn in stone grinding bins, called *metates*. Children played in the warm sun or helped with chores, while the men and boys went on hunting trips, gathered firewood, and took care of the crops of corn, beans, and squash. The haze of woodsmoke would then have filled the canyon, and the sounds of talking, laughter, singing, and the ceremonial beating of drums must have echoed from the cliffs.

A mile farther up the canyon, through groves of fragrant pines, the trail comes to Ceremonial Cave. Here the National Park Service provides a series of sturdy log ladders, so visitors may climb one hundred fifty feet up to the arched cave where archaeologists have restored a small kiva that is built into the floor of this religious retreat. Looking out over the treetops and up the canyon toward the dark summits of the Jemez Mountains, one can't help wondering what sacred rituals were performed there, and what kinds of problems the clansmen were called upon to resolve.

For about three centuries the Indians of Frijoles Canyon made their home there, as did other groups in other canyons and on the tops of mesas all across the Pajarito. Then, as at Chaco, the area was mysteriously abandoned, and new pueblos were built down by the Rio Grande. Today the Indians of Cochiti Pueblo claim that their ancestors lived in Frijoles, while other pueblos, such as San Ildefonso and Santa Clara, believe their ancestry dates back to such mesa-top sites as Tsankawi and Puyé. The Tsankawi site is protected in a separate small unit of Bandelier National Monument, while Puyé is maintained for visitors by Santa Clara Pueblo. Both pueblo sites provide magnificent panoramas of the Jemez Mountains, Pajarito Plateau, Rio Grande Valley, and the Sangre de Cristos.

One crisp late November the director of the Museum of New Mexico asked us to take an Englishman on an overnight trip to Zuñi Pueblo, in far western New Mexico, to witness an incredible, ancient religious ceremony—the *Shalako*. We arrived late in the afternoon, as the sunlight was casting long shadows on the nearby pink and white mesas. We had our first brief glimpse of the six impressive, ten-foot-tall masked *Shalako* figures as they emerged at sunset from beyond the pueblo. Then for hours we waited, walking around the sprawling pueblo, trying to keep warm as the night air grew progressively colder, and watching the Indians and other visitors coming and going.

Not long after midnight the many spectators—the Zuñis, Navajos, other Pueblo Indians, and Anglos such as ourselves—crowded into the half-dozen new houses or recent additions to houses which were to be blessed by the *Shalakos*. Inside each long room a huge figure towered above the visitors jammed together on the floor. He was a compelling giant—really rather terrifying, with his bulging eyes, long black beak, upturned horns of cow or bison, a profusion of feathers atop his head and around his neck, and a flowing white kirtle that was elaborately, strikingly embroidered with red, green, and black geometric patterns.

We waited a while longer. Finally a rhythmic drumming and chanting began at the far end of the room; suddenly the *Shalako* came to life. Back and forth the figure moved, in perfect step to the beat. Now and then he ran the length of a narrow pathway kept open in the audience—clacking his great beak and swooping as he came. Miraculously the unseen man inside never faltered or missed a step, for his weeks of preparation had developed a perfect skill to impersonate faithfully the *koko*, the ancestral messenger of the gods.

Just before dawn we went outside and walked around a corner of the pueblo. There on a rooftop we saw another ceremonial figure, the *Saiyatasha* (Longhorn), chanting a prayer. We left Zuñi at sunrise as the long roll of drumming that signals the end of the night dancing echoed across the pueblo.

The land of the Zuñis was the destination of the first major Spanish expedition into New Mexico in 1540. Having heard rumors of cities of fabulous wealth in gold and silver, the viceroy of New Spain (now Mexico) appointed his friend, Francisco Vásquez de Coronado, son of a wealthy Spanish aristocrat, to lead more than a thousand people to find the great gleaming cities, and lay claim to the new territory and its people for the Spanish Crown. After covering a thousand miles in four and a half months, the exhausted and starving explorers finally reached what they had been led to believe would be the "Seven Cities of Cíbola," but which were actually six stone-and-earthen villages of the Zuñi Indians. A brief battle ensued at the first pueblo they reached, a place called Hawikuh. When the Indians were finally forced to surrender, they fled to nearby pueblos, leaving their food supplies for the Spaniards.

Today Hawikuh, near the New Mexico–Arizona border, is in ruins, and all the Zuñis live in the single large village where we watched the *Shalako* dance.

Coronado's historic explorers went on to discover many of the other pueblos of New Mexico, and to continue the search for the fabled cities of gold and silver. When the Spaniards reached the Rio Grande, the many pueblos were at first hospitable toward the visitors. But as demands for food and other provisions increased, trust withered, tensions mounted, and battles flared. One of the pueblo chiefs was taken captive for failing to cooperate with the Spaniards, and Coronado's chronicler, Castañeda, later wrote that "This began the want of confidence in the word of the Spaniards whenever there was talk of peace from this time on."

Other difficulties followed, as Coronado's people occupied one of the Tiguex District pueblos for the winter. By early the following spring all of the nearly sixty pueblos of that district along the middle Rio Grande had either been destroyed in battle or were forced to surrender.

The adobe ruins of one such pueblo, Kuaua, are exhibited now at the Museum of New Mexico's Coronado State Monument, near today's town of Bernalillo. It was here, some years ago, that archaeologists discovered many layers of colorful murals on the interior walls of an underground kiva. After painstakingly removing and reconstructing them, they learned that these paintings portray a variety of important pueblo religious-ceremonial activities relating to the Indians' prayers for rain, crop fertility, and success in war and hunting. Each scene illustrates a particular ceremonial dance in the plaza. The Kuaua murals are among the most significant prehistoric Indian art ever found in the Southwest, and they have helped explain something of the complex religious and ceremonial life of the Pueblo Indians today.

Two years after Coronado began his huge expedition, he reluctantly admitted his failure to discover the rumored cities of wealth, and the disheartened Spaniards retraced their way back to New Spain. Yet the explorers, for all their disappointment, had learned more about the new region than the outside world had ever known before.

In 1598 another colonizing expedition was led north by New Mexico's first official governor, Don Juan de Oñate. He had been granted authority to settle the region—at his own expense. With him came 130 families, 270 single men, 83 wagons and carts of provisions, 7,000 cattle, 3,000 sheep, and other livestock.

In mid-summer the group reached the cottonwood-shaded junction of the Chama River and the Rio Grande near today's San Juan Pueblo. Two Indian villages were located there at that time, and one of these was made available to the settlers as a temporary headquarters.

Since one of the chief purposes of claiming New Mexico for Spain was to Christianize the native peoples, the first priority of church business was to divide up the surrounding pueblo region among seven Franciscan friars, so they could begin converting the sixty thousand Indians of the ninety or so pueblos. Two years later the Spaniards moved their fledgling capital to a new site across the Rio Grande, naming it San Gabriel del Yunque.

Although San Gabriel is no longer there, one of New Mexico's most beautiful drives begins at the Rio Grande near San Juan. Here the Hispanos have small apple orchards along the Chama River, where ancient cottonwoods are reflected in water that meanders lazily back and forth across the wide sandy channel.

For several miles upstream the Chama's broad floodplain is filled with irrigated green fields and small orchards, while here and there are the typically tin-roofed adobe homes of Hispano farmers. Every now and then one sees a very old, flat-roofed adobe dwelling that has been abandoned to the wind and rain slowly crumbling back to the earth. Hemming in the valley are rolling sandy hills dotted with the dark rounded forms of junipers; and in the distance rise the great mountains that are sacred to the Indians—the Jemez to the south and the Sangre de Cristos to the east.

After passing the village of Abiquiu, once the site of an ancient Indian pueblo, the road climbs along an escarpment of red bluffs, affording a view back down the Chama. The island-filled channel of the river leads the eye to distant dark lava mesas that slope down from the Jemez Mountains. From there the road emerges onto a high grassy plain where massive pink and white sandstone cliffs wall in the north side of the open expanse, and the impressive flat-topped sentinel of Cerro Pedernal rises to the south.

Along the way is Ghost Ranch Museum, where native animals are exhibited and the U.S. Forest Service tells a story of conservation. Shortly beyond the museum a dirt road branches off on the left side of the highway toward the colorful cliffs of Chama Canyon. It ends thirteen miles later at the secluded and peaceful Benedictine Monastery of Christ in the Desert.

We have visited Christ in the Desert many times, but will always cherish our first retreat there one Thanksgiving. As we drove in over the rough road (a route not recommended when it is raining) a light snow began falling. It was almost as though a veil were closing behind us. Waking the next morning to the beautiful Gregorian chants of the monks, we looked out upon a delicate, frosted world. The cottonwoods, pinyon pines, and rabbitbrush, the church and other adobe buildings were all mantled with powdery snow. High above us the sun set the sculptured pink cliffs ablaze.

Father Aelred Wall founded the monastery in 1964, and during our earliest visits he, Father Gregory Borgstedt, and Brother Anthony Lobianco were the only monks there. It was a special treat for us to be with them when they were just getting started. There was a profound feeling of peace, Christian brotherhood, and love. In addition to their religious services throughout the day, they cared for flocks of Nubian goats and sheep, prepared the meals, and during the summer raised much of their own food in irrigated fields along the Chama.

The old flat-roofed Spanish farmhouse had been restored, and was then in use as their refectory, kitchen, chapel, and guest room—all of which opened onto a tiny enclosed patio planted with small fruit trees and flowers.

The adobe church nearby, designed by architect George Nakashima, blends with the colors and forms of the canyon walls. Inside, light from large mullioned windows shines down on a central flat stone altar. Against the brown adobe walls are arrangements of dried grasses and flower stalks, and figures of Saint John the Baptist and the Virgin Mary, simply and expressively carved from cottonwood root by Ben Ortega of Tesuque. This *santero's* religious *bultos* are derived from a very old tradition of Spanish Colonial folk art in northern New Mexico. Some of the finest examples of carved *santos* may be seen at the Museum of New Mexico's International Folk Art Museum in Santa Fe.

Since those earliest days there have been many changes at the monastery: a *convento* building now houses the library, dining room, and kitchen; the old farmhouse is now a Visitor Center and gift shop. A beautifully designed guest compound provides simple accommodations for individuals and couples (for which reservations are generally required). Fathers Aelred and Gregory have now retired, and there are several new members of the community. Visitors of all faiths continue to receive a warm welcome, and the monastery remains a place of great peace and beauty.

We first saw Acoma Pueblo, the ancient "Sky City," in the half-light of dawn. The eastern sky brightened slowly, revealing a long, low cluster of buildings lying across the top of the rocky mesa. As the sun reached the earthen village and gradually inched down the huge Rock, the whole of it was bathed in gold, in contrast with the surrounding shadowed plains. Narrow rock buttresses were dramatically sidelighted, accentuating the impression of an ancient fortress.

One of Coronado's men said of Acoma: "It is one of the strongest places we have seen, because the city is on a very high rock with a rough ascent, so that we repented having gone up to the place."

Although for years the trails to the top were very steep, today a narrow road winds up to the village. Here the visitor may park, but he must get permission to be shown through the village.

There are several narrow streets between rows of two- and three-story stone-and-mud buildings. And there are a half-dozen square kivas within these buildings. Dominating the pueblo is the imposing twin-towered church of San Estevan Rey, built between 1629 and 1641 under the direction of Fray Juan Ramirez. The hardworking Acomans hauled up from the plains below all the rocks and earth that went into the church and the *campo santo*. From thirty miles to the north they brought huge forty-foot pine logs for the roof *vigas*.

The magnificent church measures one hundred fifty feet long by forty feet wide, and rises sixty feet high on massive, ten-foot-thick walls. Inside the cool white-walled nave are a colorfully painted altar, and original exquisite paintings of the Stations of the Cross, as well as other works of art. Between the church and the adjoining *convento*, an old *zambullo* door still swings on its wooden pintle hinge, with top and bottom pegs that fit into lintel and threshold sockets.

Outside in the brilliant morning sun we stood looking out over distant mesas and mountains. The sweet aroma of juniper smoke permeated the air. We became completely absorbed in the serenity and simple beauty of Acoma. It was hard to conceive of the violence that shattered the lives of the pueblo people here nearly four centuries ago.

Only a few months after the founding of San Gabriel on the Rio Grande, Governor Oñate's efforts to win the allegiance of the pueblos to the Spanish Crown and Christianity started running into trouble. As Juan de Zaldívar and his soldiers arrived at Acoma, they assumed that they would be treated hospitably. But the Indians attacked suddenly, without any apparent provocation, and killed Zaldívar and many of his men—some of whom jumped or fell from the cliff top. Zutucapan, one of the Acoma chiefs, instigated the attack because he had heard rumors that his people would be enslaved and abused by the Spaniards. This was already beginning to happen at other pueblos.

Shortly thereafter Governor Oñate ordered Vicente de Zaldívar, the slain man's brother, to lead a military attack of retribution against the Acomans. In a horrible three-day battle on the Rock the Spaniards finally succeeded in overwhelming the pueblo people—after killing nearly eight hundred of them, burning part of the village, and capturing another six hundred. Among the harsh punishments ordered by Oñate, all males over twenty-five years of age were to have one foot cut off and to give twenty years of service to the Spaniards, and males between twelve and twenty-five, and all women, were to become slaves.

Only a few families remain on the Rock today. Most of these farming people now live at or near Acomita, a few miles to the north.

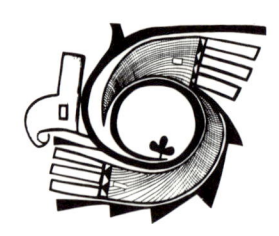

Midway between Acoma and Zuñi pueblos rises a striking headland of rock named El Morro. Steeped in history, this massive landmark has been called "America's First Guest Book." Carved into the rock are early Indian petroglyphs that portray mountain sheep and geometric designs. Governor Oñate, camping at the base of El Morro on his return from an expedition to the Gulf of California, carved an inscription into the whitish sandstone with the tip of his sword, which, translated, says:

> Passed by here the Governor Don Juan de Oñate from
> discovery of the Sea of the South on the 16th of April 1605.

Over the centuries many other names and messages have been carved into the two-hundred-foot-high headland. It is now protected within El Morro National Monument.

When Governor Oñate returned to San Gabriel from his journey by way of El Morro, he received word from the King of Spain that because of his abusive treatment of the native Indians, he was fired from his job and ordered to leave New Mexico. In his place Don Pedro de Peralta was appointed to continue the struggling colony, and to provide greater help and protection for the Franciscan missionaries. He was also ordered to find a better location for the colonial capital.

In 1610 the Spaniards moved from San Gabriel to the foothills of the Sangre de Cristos, to establish *La Villa Real de la Santa Fe de San Francisco de Assisi;* or simply, Santa Fe. One of the first adobe buildings they erected was a complex of government structures, the *"casas reales,"* part of which came to be known as the Palace of the Governors. Until 1900 this oldest public building in America served as office (and for many, as residence) for ninety-seven Spanish, Mexican, and United States governors of New Mexico. Although the front façade has been altered several times, the long portico remains, facing the central plaza. Indians from some of the nearby pueblos often gather there to sell jewelry, homemade bread, and pottery.

Santa Fe is certainly the most unusual state capital in the country. Many of its beautiful homes, churches, and commercial buildings are built of adobe, either in the Spanish-and-pueblo or Territorial architectural style. The city zoning code regulates the protection of old buildings and the design of new ones in the historic downtown district, and illuminated outdoor signs are prohibited.

Many people have moved to Santa Fe because they are able to lead quiet and creative lives while retaining their privacy. This feeling is symbolized by the high adobe walls that surround most of the homes and compounds. Painters have art galleries and studios throughout the city, notably along historic Canyon Road. Old Sena Plaza's patio is full of flowers and trees, and the front portal is lined with small shops.

At one corner of the tree-shaped plaza is the adobe-style La Fonda, an intriguing hotel built by the Santa Fe Railway to replace an old one-story inn that had long been at the end of the Santa Fe Trail.

Across the street from La Fonda rises the imposing French Romanesque Cathedral of Saint Francis, built from 1869 to 1886, under the direction of Jean Baptiste Lamy, New Mexico's beloved first archbishop. At Christmastime the old church echoes with the beautiful, colorful *mariachis* Mass, while outside, rows of candle-lighted paper bags called *luminarias* (or more accurately termed *farolitos*) festively outline many of the downtown buildings and homes of Santa Fe.

A block from the cathedral is another Lamy landmark—the little Gothic Chapel of Our Lady of Light, which for many years served the Sisters of Loretto. Copied after La Sainte-Chapelle in Paris, it is world famous for its exquisite wooden circular stairway that was built without nails and stands without any visible means of support. A further mystery is that no one has ever known who built the staircase, for the carpenter disappeared as quickly as he had come, without even waiting to be paid.

Although the Sisters of Loretto property was sold to a commercial venture in 1971, and other buildings nearby have been torn down, the chapel will be preserved as a religious shrine by the Historic Santa Fe Foundation.

Outside of Santa Fe, on the Taos highway, is the beautiful open-air Opera House, designed in adobe style, where guests may enjoy the music of artists from all over the world against a backdrop of sky and distant mountains.

Three years before New Mexico became a state in 1912, the territorial legislature founded the Museum of New Mexico, now located in four separate buildings.

The Palace of the Governors exhibits various phases of New Mexico history, while behind its patio is the Hall of the Modern Indian. The Fine Arts Museum, across the street, is a magnificent adobe-style building that incorporates architectural elements of a half-dozen Indian pueblo mission churches. It displays works of early Taos and Santa Fe painters and sculptors, as well as the more abstract art of contemporary New Mexicans.

Up on the juniper-pinyon pine foothills, just off Old Santa Fe Trail, is the museum's Laboratory of Anthropology. Built in the 1930s by the famous architect John Gaw Meem, it houses extensive collections of pottery, several exhibition rooms, a library, and research facilities. Next door is the Museum of International Folk Art, featuring fascinating exhibits of material from all over the world.

Down the hill from the latter two buildings is the privately owned Museum of Navaho Ceremonial Art, the only one of its kind, exhibiting sandpaintings, rugs, and jewelry.

During several decades after the founding of Santa Fe, the Franciscans established missions and supervised the construction of churches at many of the pueblos. As at Acoma, the Indians performed the labor, essentially following their traditional methods of construction—building with stone where that was readily available, or with adobe in places such as the middle Rio Grande Valley.

The ruins of a few of these churches, at pueblos now long abandoned, have been excavated, stabilized, and partially restored, and are now protected either by the National Park Service or the Museum of New Mexico.

Outstanding among these is Mission San José de los Jemez, dating from 1621 to 1622 and set amid the fantastic scenery of red-walled Jemez Canyon. The church's thick walls were built of red sandstone. The roof is now gone, and one may look through the front doorway and see the eight-sided lookout tower that rises forty-two feet high at the rear of the building. At one side are the remains of the walls of the *convento*, whose rooms were built around an inner patio. The mission served Giusewa Pueblo, which was abandoned later in the century because of persistent destructive attacks by marauding Indian tribes.

A trip southeast of Albuquerque, beyond the Manzano Mountains, brings the visitor to three more early missions. We made this loop tour in March one year, when the air had just a hint of spring and the sky was filled with the gracefully streamlined forms of wind clouds.

Our first stop was Quarai State Monument, located at the southeastern edge of the juniper-covered Manzanos. Massive thick red sandstone walls of Mission La Purísima Concepción, the low remnants of the *convento* and Quarai Pueblo rise from a grassy meadow. The church was built in the 1630s, and the setting, near an old grove of cottonwoods, is hauntingly beautiful.

Quarai and the other missions at nearby pueblos of Abó (Abó State Monument) and Las Humanas (Gran Quivira National Monument) sustained such devastating losses of life and property from repeated attacks by Plains Indians that the remaining inhabitants finally abandoned their villages and churches in the 1670s, and moved to other pueblos in the Rio Grande Valley that were near today's town of Socorro.

The ruins of a fifth pueblo, known as Cicuyé or Pecos, lies to the north in the Pecos River Valley, just south of the Sangre de Cristo Mountains. At the time of Coronado's expedition in 1540, Pecos was the largest of all New Mexico's Indian villages. In Castañeda's words:

> Cicuyé is a village of nearly five hundred warriors, who are feared throughout that country. It is square, situated on a rock, with a large court or plaza in the middle, containing *estufas* [kivas]. The houses are all alike, four stories high. One can walk on the roofs of the whole village, there being no streets to hinder. . . . The houses do not have doors below, but they use ladders, which can be lifted up like a drawbridge. . . . The people of this village boast that no one has been able to conquer them. . . . Their customs are like those of other villages. The maidens here, as in the others, go about naked until they take a husband. . . . [The women] wear white blankets, which cover them from the shoulders to the feet. . . . They make much of the hair and always have it

well combed, gazing at themselves in a cup of water as in a mirror.

In the early 1620s the Franciscans directed the construction of a large adobe church at Pecos Pueblo. The architecture of Mission de Neustra Señora de los Angeles de Porciuncula must have rivaled that of the great pueblo itself, for a friar described it as a "splendid temple of distinguished workmanship and beauty."

But even the undefeated Pecos finally succumbed, as did the other especially vulnerable pueblos along the edge of the Great Plains, and the few remaining people moved to Jemez Pueblo in 1838. Today the ruins are protected within Pecos National Monument.

The first director of the Museum of New Mexico, Dr. Edgar L. Hewett, once said that "These five churches [Jemez, Quarai, Abó, Gran Quivira, and Pecos] . . . constitute a noble group of ruins . . . crude, massive, elemental as compared with the later missions of California, Arizona, and Texas . . . a style not dependent upon ornamentation for its distinction but resting its claim of merit solely upon a . . . formal tradition that perfectly meets the requirements of a unique, elemental environment."

Later in the seventeenth century, as the Franciscans continued to spread Christianity, friction developed between the clergy and public officials. Charges and countercharges were hurled back and forth. There were complaints that civilian and military authorities were abusing the Pueblo Indians and forcing them to become unpaid servants. Government officials alleged that the Church was interfering with the affairs of State, and that religious leaders were often inflicting cruel punishment, such as whipping, imprisonment, and even death, upon Indians refusing to give up their ancient religious beliefs and observances.

In the midst of the controversies the Indians of several pueblos plotted now and then to overthrow the Spaniards. These attempts were all foiled, until the summer of 1680. The patient and long-suffering Indians finally unleashed decades of resentment. They killed some four hundred Spaniards, and forced two thousand others to flee for their lives.

Twelve years later, 1692, a new Spanish leader, a tall, proud aristocrat named Don Diego de Vargas, led the colonists back into New Mexico—which, an inscription at El Morro says, he "conquered for our Holy Faith, and for the Royal Crown at his own expense."

In 1706 the next governor, Don Francisco Cuervo y Valdes, founded the city of Albuquerque. Although today's high-rise buildings and urban sprawl overshadow what remains of the early settlement, Old Town still preserves some of the charm of old adobe buildings that were erected on the original land grant designated by the King of Spain. One of the first structures was the Church of San Felipe de Neri. All of the original edifice is believed to have been destroyed late in the eighteenth century. The present church building dates from 1793.

Because of the danger of raids by Navajos, Comanches, and Apaches, many of the early Spanish villages were built as small forts. Sun-baked Plaza del Cerro, founded in the 1730s, is located just off the main road through Chimayó. You can easily drive right by, as we did the first several times, without ever realizing it is there. It took the help of a village priest to direct us to the narrow opening into the plaza, around which the old adobe buildings are built wall-to-wall. Originally the outer wall of the community had no doors or windows, to reduce further the opportunity of attack from outside.

The plaza is really a little world unto itself, with *acequias* running this way and that, bringing the water for plots of corn and chili peppers. Bright orange and yellow flowers provide accents of color against the brown adobe walls. As we walked about enjoying the tranquillity, an elderly Hispano paused a moment in his hammering of a fence and greeted us with a friendly *"Buenos dias!"* Farther on, a large dog fiercely barked disapprovingly at our intrusion.

Since the founding of the walled village, Chimayó has spread across the surrounding area—with tin-roofed adobe houses, garden plots, and little fruit orchards scattered here and there. For many years Chimayó has been famous for the weaving of high-quality wool blankets—a craft that may still be observed in a number of the Hispanic mountain villages of northern New Mexico.

Another historic landmark in Chimayó is the little twin-towered adobe chapel, El Santuario. Built in 1816, it served as a private chapel for more than a century, until it was saved from ruin and given to the Catholic Church. When we last stopped there, an artist was seated out front, hard at work with paints and canvas beneath her broad-brimmed straw hat.

From Chimayó we have frequently taken the paved road up into the rolling foothills of the Sangre de Cristos to visit other mountain villages tucked away from the mainstream of modern life. One of the most interesting along the way is Truchas—perched atop a long windswept ridge, in full view of the craggy Truchas Peaks. It is a picturesque scene of old homes, stores, log barns, corrals, and a *morada*. The *morada*, with small windows and a tiny steeple, is one of the many brotherhood houses or chapels scattered throughout northern New Mexico where the Penitente Brotherhood have long held their secret religious ceremonies. The Penitentes, who were most active during the nineteenth and early twentieth centuries, and who still have a few followers in some of the remote villages, are especially remembered for their religious custom of self-flagellation and related acts of torture. These harsh means of achieving grace are vividly described by Charles F. Lummis in his 1893 classic, *The Land of Poco Tiempo*.

Truchas is a simple place yet beautiful in its simplicity, in its closeness to the land. Especially interesting are the weaving shops, where brightly colored rugs, shoulder bags, and serapes are skillfully woven on the old looms. The weavers there are justly proud of an old tradition that has been passed down from generation to generation. One is not surprised to find such talent in the villages of New Mexico. These little timeless things, both natural and man-made, keep appearing unexpectedly, to make this state so unusually fascinating.

The road from Truchas continues northward, over pine-covered ridges and into little valleys where other Hispanic villages nestle among fields and garden plots. One of these tiny, hidden places is called Las Trampas.

In 1751 a seventy-four-year-old Santa Fean named Juan de Arguello moved to this secluded valley with eleven families, and—in spite of threats of Indian raids—founded Las Trampas on a forty-six-thousand-acre land grant from the Spanish Crown. Like those in the plaza of Chimayó, the houses were originally built wall-to-wall around a spacious plaza. Not all the buildings are still standing, but one can visualize how it was.

In the early 1760s construction of an adobe lay chapel was begun. Today the church of San José de Garcia de las Trampas is one of the most beautiful and authentic examples of early Spanish Colonial church architecture in New Mexico. It is so significant, in fact, that a public furor resulted when a highway straightening project in 1966 threatened to sheer off part of the church yard and come within a mere six feet of the church itself. A successful campaign of opposition to the highway proposal was spearheaded by the internationally known architect, Nathaniel A. Owings. In 1967 the U.S. Department of the Interior designated the church and surrounding area as a National Historic Landmark. And finally, a group calling itself Las Trampas Foundation raised funds to repair the building—with the villagers themselves performing the labor. A new roof was laid over the ancient *vigas*, and the exterior of the church was replastered with a new layer of adobe mud. As Owings described it in *New Mexico* magazine:

> What a sight that was, those . . . assured, competent
> women each settling to her special task—one the sifting of the
> specially selected adobe earth, one to sort . . . shred and mix
> the strands of straw, another adding the proper amount of
> water and digging in, elbow deep, to mix the plastic substance
> to the right consistency. They were constantly supplied with
> mud and water and straw by the men. . . .
> The application of the adobe, the amount of moisture
> applied to the surface before application—everything is done
> truly, a chain reaction of an ancient tradition.

Already the wind, rain, melting snow, and baking sun have begun to erode and mold the surface of the old church, so that it blends even more fully with the land from which it came. Someday the villagers will join together again to renew the church, and with it, their own sense of unity with each other and with the earth.

Beyond Las Trampas the road comes to a junction in the valley of el Rio Pueblo. Upstream the road (State Route 3) follows one of the most pleasant wild stream valleys in the Sangre de Cristos—where the clear sparkling water dashes along beneath tall pines, firs, and cottonwoods, and meanders through meadows carpeted with wildflowers in summer and autumn.

Turning downstream at the junction from Las Trampas, the road comes shortly to a fork to the right which leads into the little farming valley of Picurís— the only Indian pueblo located in the mountains. From a distance the brown clusters of houses blend with the land, while its whitewashed church catches the eye.

For four hundred years this tiny pueblo has been famous for handmade undecorated bean pots and pitchers that sparkle with flecks of mica in the clay. Often the pottery has such thin walls and is so well fired that it rings when tapped. Only a few of the more elderly women are potters and it seems sadly inevitable that one day Picurís will no longer be known for its outstanding micaceous ware.

At many other pueblos pottery is an important source of pride, as well as revenue. Originally the Indians made pots, bowls, pitchers, and great storage *ollas* for their utilitarian needs. Each pueblo became known for its own distinctive ceramic art—some of the finest of which was done during the nineteenth and early twentieth centuries. Stylized bird motifs have been among the most common decorations in ceramic art. Acoma, Zuñi, Zía, and San Ildefonso pots display particularly striking "winged messengers," while Zuñi pots also often display a characteristic arrangement of deer with the red "life line" that runs from the mouth to an arrow at the heart. Cochiti potters have used a variety of religiously significant fertility symbols, such as clouds and rain. And Santo Domingo has been known for bold geometric patterns.

Visiting some of the Indian pueblos is a rewarding experience. Zía was the first I had been to. It was dusk, and from a short distance away I could hardly tell there was a village up on the top of a small rocky promontory. Every bit of the limited space is taken by wall-to-wall rows of stone-and-mud houses, a small dance plaza, little alleyways, several beehive-shaped adobe ovens, and the ancient church. (Zía, as well as many other pueblos, does not permit visitors to use cameras.)

At Cochiti Pueblo, along the Rio Grande, just below the mouth of White Rock Canyon where a dam is now being built, I had my first taste of Indian bread. It was fascinating to watch the women build a fire inside an adobe oven, then scrape out the hot coals and lay in variously shaped mounds of dough with a long-handled flat paddle. The browned bread that emerged a while later was some of the most delicious I have ever eaten anywhere.

To the north, near Black Mesa, is the pueblo of San Ildefonso. It is a village long known for exceptional artistic talent, but made especially famous by the potter María, whose perfectly shaped handmade pottery has brought her world recognition. For many years, until their deaths, María's husband, Julian Martínez, and then her son, Popovi-Da, worked together on the black-on-black glazed bowls and other pottery—she shaping and smoothing the clay, and her husband or son painting the designs before it was fired.

I miss Popovi-Da when I visit San Ildefonso now. When he was at his pueblo gift shop, I always found him a most pleasant, kindly man, his dark eyes full of wisdom. When we first met, we laughed in learning that both our names translated to mean "Red Fox." Above my desk is a black-on-black bowl which I treasure. On the bottom it is signed, "María" and "Popovi-Da."

The pueblos of New Mexico are all unique in their culture and physical settings. Many Indians have jobs in Santa Fe or other cities, but they still follow much of their ancient religious ceremonial traditions.

We have watched a number of the sacred ceremonial dances including, most memorably, a Buffalo Dance one crisp Christmas Day at Cochiti, and a midsummer Corn Dance under the blazing sun at Santa Ana.

As we waited in the cool shade of a big cottonwood at Santa Ana for the beginning of the dance for summer rain and crop fertility, the stillness of the dry, hot air was suddenly broken by deep drum beats and a low musical chanting. The dancers had climbed out of their kiva and were filing in two long lines onto the plaza, where spectators were backed against the adobe walls.

The men were bare to the waist and dressed in embroidered white kirtles, each tied with a tasseled white rain sash. In their right hands they held dry gourd rattles which they shook to the throbbing rhythm. Their moccasined feet emphatically stamped the hard-packed earth, each step jangling the strings of shells around their necks and rattles tied below their knees.

The women were barefooted, delicately shuffling to the compelling beat, keeping close to the earth, that all life might be filled with the idea of fertility. They wore black *mantas* which they had tied about the waist with red and green woven sashes. Wooden *tablitas* on their heads were painted the color of the sky and carved into stylized shapes of clouds and mesas. In their hands were small pieces of fir branches which they swayed gently to the drum beat.

At the head of the lines of dancers was a man bearing a tall pole. Clusters of red feathers fluttered from the top, along with a fox's tail and a banner embroidered with the motifs of rain. Dipping and swaying above the dancers' heads, the pole represented the sun's fertility, tempting the rain to come.

From time to time the drummer, chanters, and dancers skipped a beat and then a second—all in perfect unison. On and on went the rhythm and movement of the dance, until the pulsating waves of sound enveloped us, seeming to draw down the pulsating heat of the sun itself. This spectacular ceremony continued all day, with two groups, representing the pueblo's two moieties, taking turns. Every chant and movement and every part of the ceremonial costumes was directed toward placating the supernatural forces, bringing the people of the pueblo into harmony with nature, and invoking the sustenance of all life—water.

As Peggy Pond Church says in her extraordinarily perceptive book, *The House at Otowi Bridge:*

> The Pueblos have always believed that the earth they live upon is sacred. Each stone and bush and tree is alive with a spirit like their own. . . . [They] have established a moving relationship with the land they dwell in. They live in community not only with each other, but with earth and sky, with plants and animals. They consciously play their part in maintaining the wholeness of the universe; wholeness or holiness— it is more than a play on words. It is the recognition of the common spirit that animates all life.

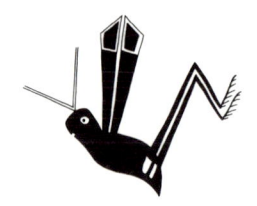

When the United States purchased the vast Louisiana Territory from France in 1803, a flood of trappers, traders, and government-sponsored expeditions began pouring west. Most of those who first ventured into virtually unknown New Mexico, however, were treated by Spanish officials as trespassers, and were either jailed or promptly sent back to the United States.

Only after 1821, when Mexico, including her provinces of New Mexico, California, and Texas, declared independence from Spain, were Americans tolerated and even welcomed. In that same year William Becknell, with seventy companions and a string of pack horses, came across the Great Plains from Missouri and struggled over Raton Pass into New Mexico. Upon reaching Santa Fe they were enthusiastically greeted, and the residents quickly bought up all their American merchandise.

Becknell was so encouraged that he returned the following year with three wagon loads of goods; and two years later with the first wagon train of twenty-four wagons and eighty traders, laden with clothing, textiles, food, cutlery, hardware, and even furniture—thus founding the Santa Fe Trail.

The volume of trade quickly grew and business boomed. Commonly there were a hundred wagons per train and several million dollars' worth of business annually. At the Trail's end long lines of covered wagons crowded around the central plaza of Santa Fe, in front of the Palace of the Governors—creating a situation that drew an indignant response from the local newspaper, *The New Mexican*, on October 18, 1872:

> The streets of Santa Fe were never so dirty as now. Hay
> wagons, bull trains, etc., have been camping about the plaza
> for more than a week, adding all their filth to the already
> abundant dust, until the public square presents a shameful
> appearance. . . . Trains must unload about the plaza, but we

object to their camping or waiting for sales, about it. Let us see
some measures taken, to prevent making a barnyard of the
heart of the city.

One may still visit some of the old stage stops along the Santa Fe Trail in northeastern New Mexico, such as Wagon Mound, at the base of a volcanic mountain that was a key landmark to travelers, or Watrous, in the heart of cattle ranching country along the Mora River, and San Miguel del Vado.

San Miguel, where the wagon trains forded the Pecos River, was for many years a bustling customs collection stop for the Mexican regime in Santa Fe. But when the Santa Fe Railway between Raton Pass and Albuquerque bypassed San Miguel in 1879, the town's population rapidly declined. Today many of the old adobe buildings are crumbling into ruin.

At the same time that ties with Mexico were weakening, the Santa Fe Trail created a strong economic link between New Mexico and the United States. It was almost inevitable that political and military union should follow. Thus when Colonel Stephen W. Kearny entered New Mexico in 1846 with eighteen hundred troops, the United States was able to take possession of the territory without even firing a shot.

New Mexico had a brief encounter with the Civil War, during 1861 and 1862, when an army of Confederates was defeated by soldiers from Fort Union and volunteers from the Colorado gold mines. The U.S. military then turned its full attention to subduing the marauding Indian tribes, whose destructive raids had for so long plagued the Spanish and Mexican governments of New Mexico. These and other U.S. military events which took place in New Mexico are described by the exhibits at the Fort Union National Monument Visitor Center, near the ruins of the once powerful military headquarters.

In 1862 Colonel Kit Carson, already famous as a trapper and guide, was sent with troops to defeat the Mescalero Apaches in their rugged territory around Sierra Blanca Peak and in the Sacramento Mountains of southern New Mexico. The orders he received said that "All Indian men of that tribe are to be killed whenever and wherever you can find them. The women and children will not be harmed, but you will take them prisoners. . . ." Many Indians were killed in a three-pronged attack into the rugged Sacramentos. Survivors pleaded that ". . . we are worn out; . . . your troops are everywhere. . . . You have driven us from our last and best stronghold, and we have no more heart." By early 1863 over four hundred of them were held captive on the bleak Bosque Redondo Reservation along the Pecos River, guarded by soldiers from nearby Fort Sumner.

Eventually many of the Indians escaped, and today part of that "last and best stronghold" is the Apache's Mescalero Reservation, where cattle and timber are important means of livelihood. On the slopes of Sierra Blanca's North Ridge the Indians have developed a ski area with a modern lodge, ski lifts rising to over eleven thousand feet above sea level, and twenty-three miles of ski trails. The road up to the resort switchbacks through high mountain forests of the Lincoln National Forest, from one breathtaking view to another across the surrounding mountains and plains. In autumn, along the slopes, the yellow and rust of the aspens and oaks contrast with the dark greens of the pines and Douglas firs.

In spite of Carson's success in crushing the Mescalero Apaches, the governor of New Mexico reported to the legislature in 1863: "It is my disagreeable duty to again repeat that our Territory still suffers from the hostility of the Indian tribes which surround us. . . . Our losses in life and property by these tribes have been greater than ever before. . . ."

Carson and his troops were next dispatched to northwestern New Mexico to force the surrender of the Navajos. After destroying much of their livestock and crops, he finally captured many of the Indians in Arizona's Canyon de Chelly, and marched them three hundred miles southeast to the Bosque Redondo. More than eight thousand Navajos were ultimately held there, suffering the humility of exile, hunger, crop failures, and many deaths, until finally, four years later, the tribe signed a peace treaty. In 1868, under its terms, they were allowed to return to their homeland. They have remained peaceful ever since.

Today, the Navajos are the largest Indian tribe in the United States, totaling about one hundred thousand people. Their reservation is a vast arid region, sprawling across northwestern New Mexico and parts of adjacent Arizona and Utah. On one of our visits to the area we drove down the San Juan River, its broad, irrigated valley lush with green fields, and then turned south from the dusty town of Shiprock.

For miles there the road crosses bleak, brown treeless plains, where jagged volcanic formations, such as Shiprock and Bennett Peak, jut up boldly. Scattered here and there are hogans, little six- or eight-sided log dwellings that have long been characteristic of the Navajo landscape. Occasionally we passed a horse-drawn wagon or buckboard crossing the highway to follow a dirt track across the desert expanse. Amid the solitude of earth and sky, lone shepherds wandered with flocks of sheep whose thick wool is much prized by the Navajos for making rugs.

One of the objectives of our trip was to find a Navajo weaver. So with hope we turned off toward the dark ridge of the pine-covered Chuska Mountains that lay to the west against the Arizona border, and soon came to the village of Toadlena. After inquiring at a local mission, we found the home of Mrs. Fanny Deal. She and her mother were looking for someone to drive them several miles into the mountains to their summer camp—a log cabin beneath tall pines. We gladly volunteered.

In a log-and-brush lean-to, against one end of the cabin, her vertical loom was set up. On it was a strikingly beautiful rug in the Two Gray Hills pattern, a third completed. Her skilled hands quickly worked the wooden comb and batten. The latter is inserted in the shed and turned to make an opening wide enough to pass the weft through; the comb is then used to tighten down the weft.

In this age of mass production the Navajo women still clean, card, spin, and dye their wool by hand. The colors of the bold symmetrical patterns of Two Gray Hills rugs are obtained from black, brown, and white wool, which they also blend to produce various shades of gray and tan. The soft earth colors of other prized styles of Navajo rugs, such as Wide Ruin and Crystal, are made from the vegetable dyes of such native plants as juniper root and berries, sagebrush, globemallow, sunflower, penstemon, purple beeplant, and snakeweed.

It is amazing that the Navajos create so much beauty in such a difficult land. It is also amazing, in the face of change and the pressure of outside influences, that they still retain many of their ancient sacred beliefs and traditions.

Whereas nearly all Pueblo Indian religious observances are performed mainly to bring the entire *community* into harmony with the universe, the main emphasis in many of the most important Navajo ceremonies is to bring the *individual* into harmony with the universe—to restore and maintain his or her health.

Curing ceremonies, or "medicine chants," involve many days of sacred rituals performed by Navajo medicine men, and they include the creation of elaborate sandpaintings and the singing of prayers. Some of these events climax with public night dances acted by masked impersonators of the deities of Navajo mythology, the *Yeibichai*.

Great numbers of Navajos travel far across the reservation to attend these ceremonies, the women wearing their traditional long flowing skirts and colorful velvet blouses adorned with turquoise or silver squash-blossom necklaces. The men, in cowboy-style outfits with handsome handmade silver buckles on their belts, commonly wear tall, broad-brimmed black hats.

But there are changes. The versatile pickup truck has largely replaced the horse and wagon, a modern house often sits next door to the old hogan, and tribal revenues are being enhanced by the exploitation of oil, gas, and coal resources beneath the wind-swept land.

Minerals have long been important in New Mexico. Early Spaniards used Indian labor to work gold deposits in the sixteenth and seventeenth centuries. High-grade copper was discovered in 1800 at Santa Rita. From there it was sent on mules to Mexico City for coinage at the Royal Mint. Today Santa Rita has become Kennecott Copper Corporation's gigantic one-thousand-foot-deep, one-and-a-half-mile-wide open pit mine.

In 1828 gold was discovered in the Ortiz Mountains, about thirty miles southwest of Santa Fe, setting off the first major gold rush in America. Eight years later coal also was discovered in those mountains, initiating the first recorded coal mining in the West, and turning a place called Madrid into a boom town.

In the beautiful Moreno Valley, on the opposite side of the Sangre de Cristos from Taos, mining fever, first over copper and then over gold, began in 1866. But you wouldn't know it today. All that remain of once-flourishing Elizabethtown are a few little clapboard houses and the crumbling stone walls of the old Mutz Hotel.

Thousands of people poured into the valley during those rollicking years, and millions of dollars in gold were scraped and dug from the land. Within a year of its founding, "E-town" boasted seven saloons, two hotels, several dance halls, many stores, and a newspaper. In the frenzied atmosphere there were brawls and murders, and vigilantes were organized to stop the violence.

Another deceptively peaceful ghost town is White Oaks, dating from 1879. Little remains of this town tucked away in the juniper hills near Carrizozo—but there is a tall, stately red brick Victorian mansion, called "Hoyle's Castle," that was lavishly built by a man for a bride-to-be who decided not to marry him after all. Fronting on what was once the mile-long main street of this town of four thousand people are the crumbling remains of a couple of old stores and scores of weed-filled cellar holes.

At the western edge of the rugged Mogollon Mountains, in southwestern New Mexico, a narrow paved road runs across a grassy plateau, winds over a little mountain pass, and descends abruptly to one of the state's most famous ghost towns—Mogollon. Rough old stores and houses line the winding main street along Silver Creek, and the decaying foundations of many other houses and shacks march up the steep hillsides.

Only a few residents still live in Mogollon, where once there were more than two thousand people during the boom era from the 1880s to 1915. As much as three million dollars' worth of gold and silver ore was extracted annually. Just over the ridge from Mogollon, the Little Fanney Mine's vacant corrugated steel buildings stand starkly above the white streak of tailings in the canyon below.

East of Mogollon is one of the most remote mountain regions in the United States, most of it protected within the sprawling Gila National Forest. A large part of the forest has been designated the Gila Wilderness. It is a vast unspoiled roadless area, set aside in 1924, the first place in the country devoted exclusively to wilderness preservation. Its existence is a tribute to the famous ecologist, Aldo Leopold, who promoted the idea.

Today wilderness pack trips are among the most popular use of the Gila, and there are places where horses and a guide may be hired—such as at the small store at Gila Hot Springs.

From the air the Gila country appears as an almost endless jumble of forested mountain ridges running in all directions, with the Mimbres River Valley cutting across the southeast corner, and the great gash of the Gila River slicing a tortuous course through the southwest.

It is from scattered ruins of small Indian villages along the Mimbres and upper tributaries of the Gila that archaeologists have discovered a black-on-white pottery that surpasses all other ceramic art of the prehistoric Southwest. Dating roughly from A.D. 1100 to 1300, the imaginative geometric and naturalistic designs were painted most commonly across the inside of shallow bowls. They portray stylized birds, mammals, fish, reptiles, and insects, as well as "scenes" of hunting, trapping, and ceremonial dances.

Also in the upper Gila are a few cliff dwellings dating from the late 1200s. Gila Cliff Dwellings National Monument now protects one group of them in a series of deep caves high in the walls of a narrow canyon. Although until recently this area was difficult to reach, visitors now may follow a short trail from the end of a paved road.

One of the most scenic parts of this region is Gila Canyon, the lower end of which can be reached over a rough U.S. Forest Service road—except when rains have made the route impassable. Groves of cottonwoods and fragrant white-barked Arizona sycamores shade stretches of sandy banks along the river. If you are fortunate, you may see a bald eagle soaring down the canyon. The surrounding rugged mountains leave no doubt why it took the U.S. military forces so long to subdue the last few freedom-loving bands of Apaches in the 1880s.

In a last desperate attempt to hold back the rising influx of the white man and hold onto their ancient, independent way of life, the Apaches laid down wave after wave of terror, death, and destruction, only to melt back into the rugged mountains of southwestern New Mexico and adjacent Arizona and Mexico. Even though leaders such as Victorio, Nana, Josanie, Nachez, Cochise, and Geronimo were skilled in guerrilla warfare, in the end they were harassed to sheer exhaustion by the U.S. military and forced to accept either extermination or confinement and exile. The final major surrender of the Apaches came in 1886, when Geronimo and his tattered band gave themselves up to the soldiers in Skeleton Canyon on the New Mexico–Arizona border in the rugged Peloncillo Mountains.

Another impressive New Mexico mountain area is the Pecos Wilderness, in the Santa Fe National Forest of the southern Sangre de Cristos. We backpacked in from the end of the road near Cowles on a glittering October morning, following the switchbacking trail beneath the forest of tall pines and Douglas firs. After picnicking in a grove of golden aspens, we emerged onto a high sweeping expanse of grass that afforded views of mountains in every direction. Strings of pack horses went by, loaded with camping gear for the elk-hunting season that was to begin shortly. Huge billowy thunderheads were quickly building over the rocky summits of Santa Fe Baldy and Pecos Baldy. In the gathering blackness the storm finally unleashed its fury, sending crackling bolts of lightning and booming thunder down on the peaks, and pelting us with a downpour of hail. At sunset the remaining few traces of cloud turned orange and then pink and purple.

A third wilderness area lies to the north in the Sangre de Cristos, encompassing much of the high country around New Mexico's highest point, 13,160-foot Wheeler Peak. One of the main trails to this area of little alpine lakes and tundra begins at the famed Taos Ski Valley. From the lodge in the sheltered basin skiers ride lifts 2,600 feet up the mountainsides and skim down the miles of winding ski trails.

In southeastern New Mexico, more than eight hundred feet underground, near the Guadalupe Mountains, lies one of the largest limestone caves in the world—Carlsbad Caverns. Gigantic rooms are draped and pillared with fantastic, monumental yellow, red, and brown stalactites and stalagmites. The Big Room alone encompasses fourteen acres, with a ceiling that arches more than 250 feet above the floor. The National Park Service provides a self-guiding tour that passes an endless array of formations with such names as Temple of the Sun, Niagara Falls, Giant Dome, Twin Domes, and Totem Pole.

The caverns were discovered around the turn of the century by a young miner, James Larkin White, and largely through his enthusiastic descriptions the area was declared a national monument in 1923. It was subsequently designated by Congress as a national park, and today attracts more visitors than any other natural attraction in the state.

Aboveground much of the reserve is covered with typical Chihuahuan Desert vegetation, such as lechuguilla, century plant, yuccas, sotol, ocotillo, and a few varieties of cacti. Mule deer, jackrabbits, kangaroo rats, and coyotes sometimes may be seen.

A few miles to the west along Guadalupe Ridge from the Visitor Center and Caverns entrance, a dirt road ends at the mouth of wild Slaughter Canyon. From there trails lead throughout the roadless backcountry of the park. We have taken the trail to New Cave, up the west side of the canyon, in the early morning before the sun was too hot, stopping frequently to examine the varieties of yuccas, agaves, cacti, grasses, and other plant life. We were surprised to discover, in that arid land, scattered small clumps of a fern, the fronds of which were tightly rolled to conserve moisture.

Each kind of desert plant has evolved special ways of coping with long periods of dessicating drought and intense heat. After brief periods of winter and spring rain the spiny, long-branched ocotillo puts out tiny leaves perhaps several times a year, triumphs with a grand display of reddish-orange blossoms at the end of each stalk, then sheds the leaves when the heat and drought return. Many wildflower annuals rush into bloom and produce seeds only if the winter or spring rains have been sufficient; otherwise, they lie dormant until a better year. Succulent plants such as the cacti quickly absorb rainwater through their shallow network of roots, storing the moisture in their thorn-protected fleshy stems and branches. Some, like the mesquite, have roots that reach down to permanent underground water, while creosote bush emits a toxic substance that keeps away competitors. Still others have leaves covered with a waxy coating that reduces transpiration. In endless variety, each species has devised ways to survive the harsh environment.

Another unusual area in southern New Mexico's Chihuahuan Desert is White Sands National Monument, located in the Tularosa Basin a few miles west of Alamogordo. Covering an expanse that measures roughly ten by thirty miles, the pure white sand dunes are composed of tiny particles of gypsum that prevailing southwesterly winds have carried from beds of selenite crystals on the nearby dry bed of Lake Lucero. During the flat light of midday this unique sandscape is really too intensely bright to enjoy. It is best seen either in early morning or shortly before sunset, when purple shadows accentuate the wind-sculptured crescent forms and rippled surfaces, and the tall flower stalks of the yuccas cast long shadows across the sand.

Early in the morning one can find the tracks of countless nocturnal creatures—mice, kangaroo rats, pocket gophers, ground squirrels, and beetles. We were interested to learn that some species of lizards and mice have evolved special protective coloration to blend with the white sand, making it difficult for hawks, owls, and other enemies to find them. One species of pocket mouse has even developed different-colored races: white ones at White Sands, brown ones nearby, and almost black ones that live in a lava flow a few miles to the north.

Toward the north end of that fifty-mile-long black Malpais, the highway between Carrizozo and San Antonio (near Socorro) crosses a stretch of the lava. From a camping area at Valley of Fires State Park, one may look across miles of the twisted, jumbled landscape where tall-stalked sotol, yuccas, and cholla and prickly pear cacti somehow manage to survive.

One of New Mexico's most exciting waterfowl areas—the Bosque del Apache National Wildlife Refuge—is a few miles south of Socorro. Its thousands of acres of diked ponds, marshes, and fields stretch along the Rio Grande, and from fall until spring thousands of ducks and geese flock there. Greater sandhill cranes walk about on spindly long legs or fly gracefully overhead. Coronado's expedition reported seeing these cranes along the Rio Grande in 1540, as did the early American explorer James W. Abert in 1846. Abert's report mentions big flocks that "kept up a great whooping" along the river bosques.

It was to save the great gray cranes from extinction that this refuge was established in 1939. Since then at least two hundred and seventy other species of birds have been recorded there—notably thousands of Canada and snow geese, and many species of ducks, including the rare Mexican duck.

Another major waterfowl area is Bitter Lake National Wildlife Refuge, located along the Pecos River several miles east of Roswell. This reserve not only provides the wintering habitat for a large part of the world's total population of lesser sandhill cranes, sometimes numbering as many as seventy thousand, but also has the most important concentration of ducks and geese in eastern New Mexico. The peak time is late October when the sky is filled with the flights of cranes wheeling and gliding, while all around the shallow diked lakes are flocks of snow and Canada geese, rafts of ducks, and a few large white pelicans.

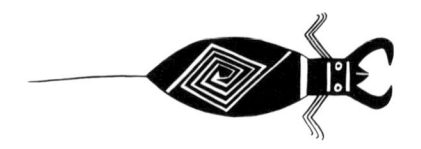

In northern New Mexico awesome Rio Grande Gorge has carved a huge winding gash into the sagebrush plains northwest of Taos. This area was the first stretch of wild river in the country set aside for protection by Congress under special wild river legislation. Its challenging white-water course is very popular with kayak enthusiasts.

An especially breathtaking view of the gorge is from the five-hundred-foot-high span of the Rio Grande Gorge Bridge (on U.S. Route 64). When one looks down on the river's foaming rapids, which are barely audible from the bridge, it is interesting to try to comprehend the flow of time—the hundreds of thousands of years it has taken nature to carve this great gorge, since the age when molten lava flows first poured from the earth and cooled and hardened into rock. The river has been flowing within these sheer walls while man hunted mammoths and mastodons, lived in pithouses, built great stone pueblos, and eventually established the tri-culture civilization that is now New Mexico.

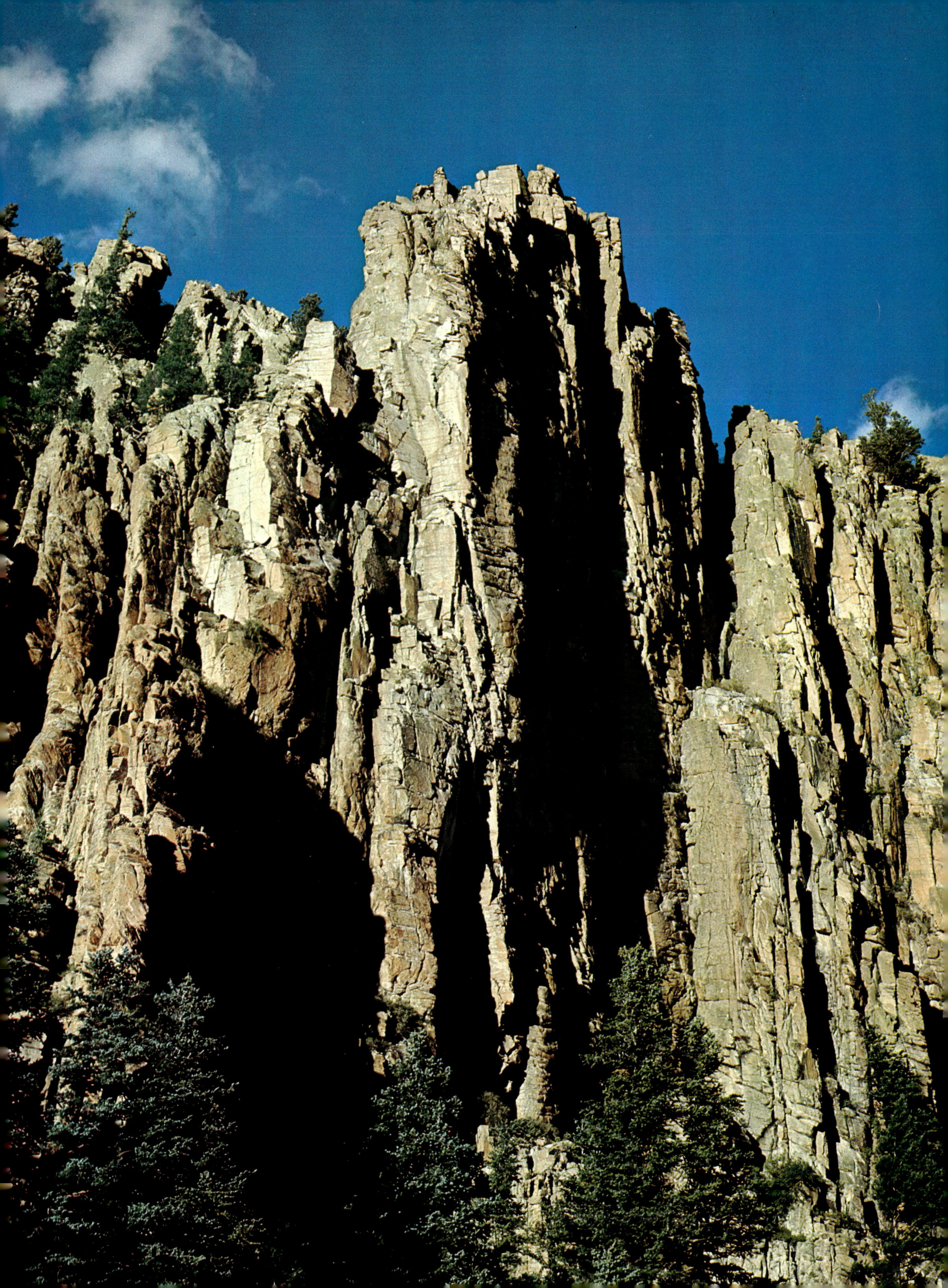

2

3

4

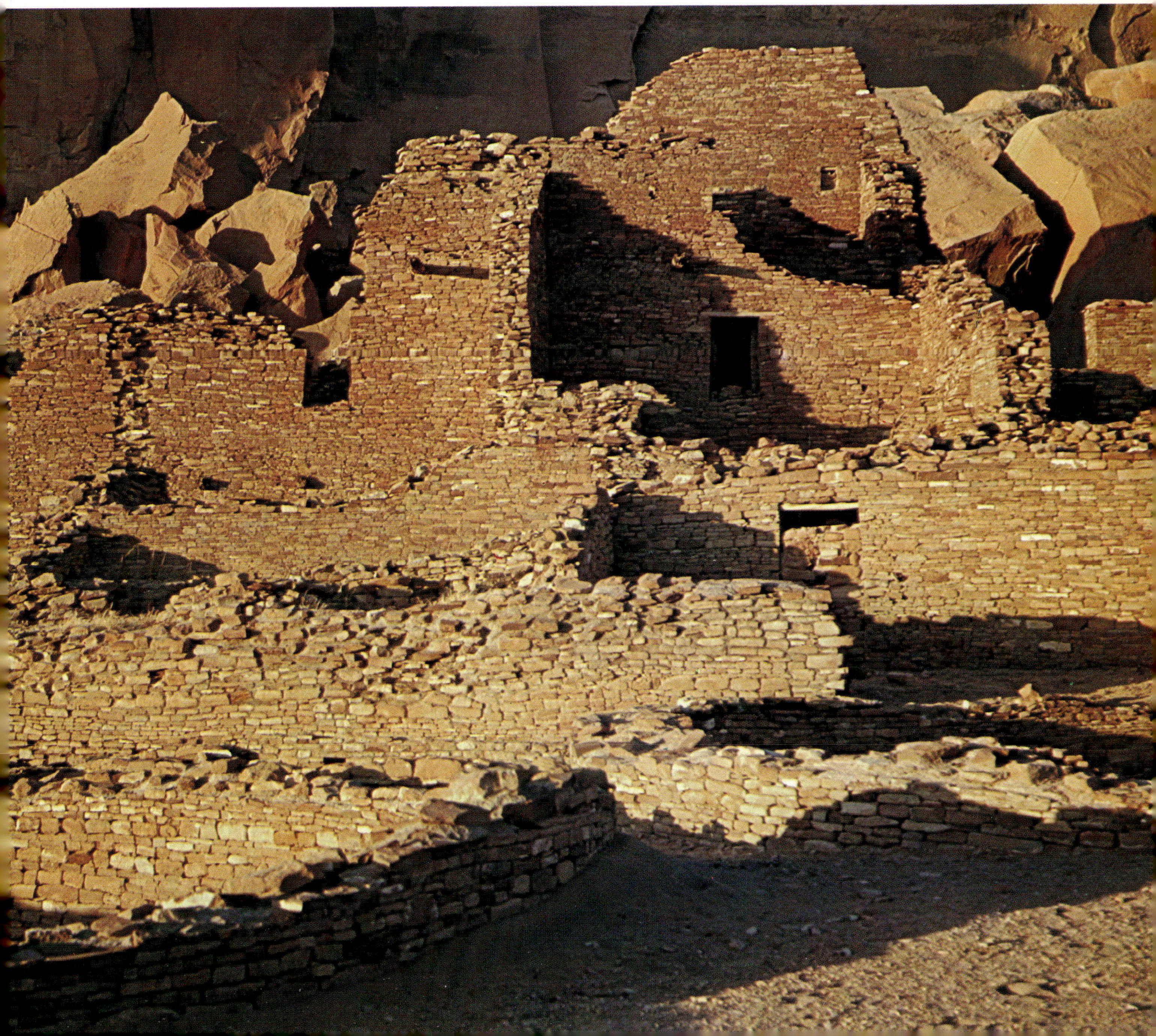

5

6

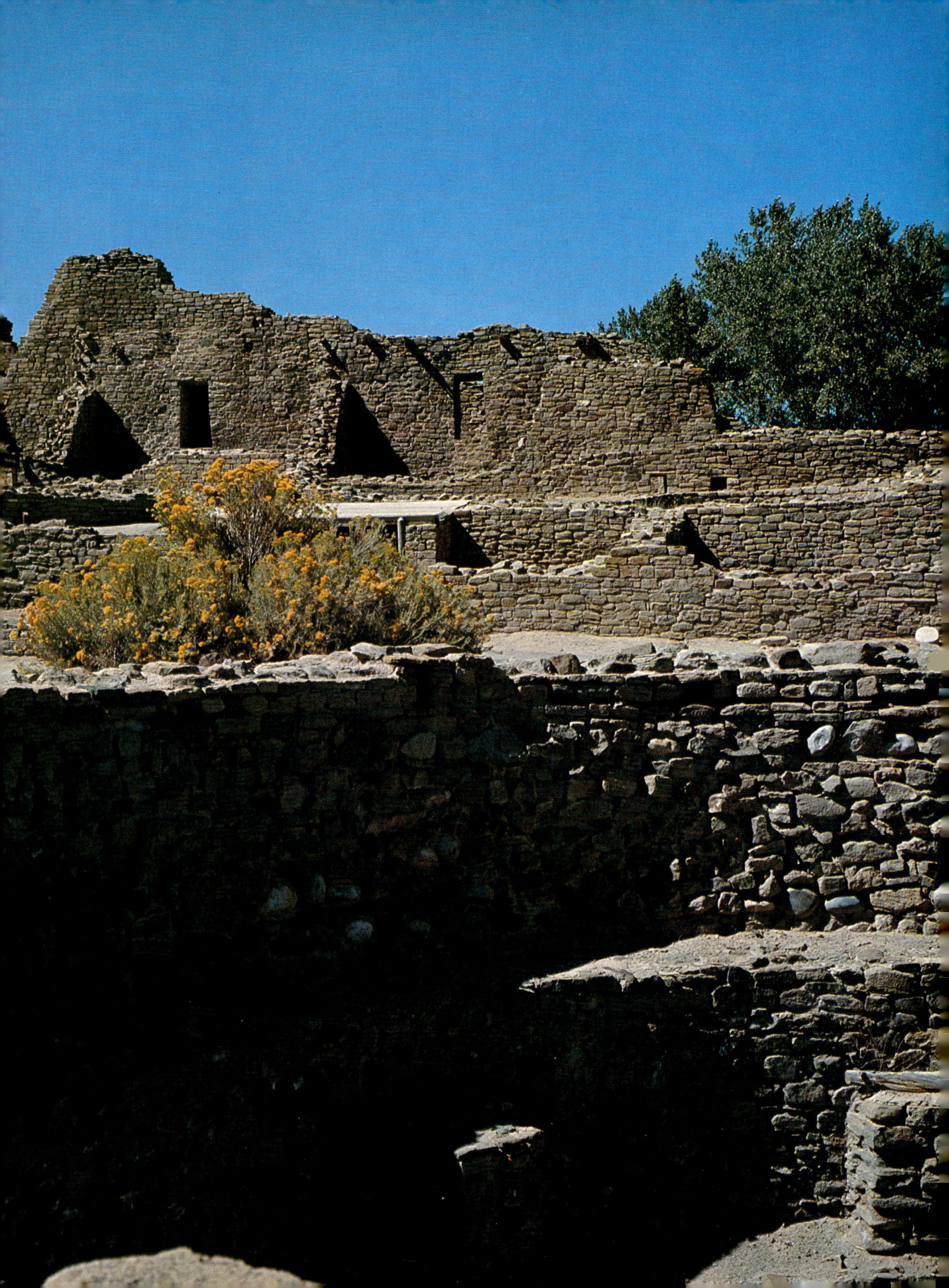

7

8

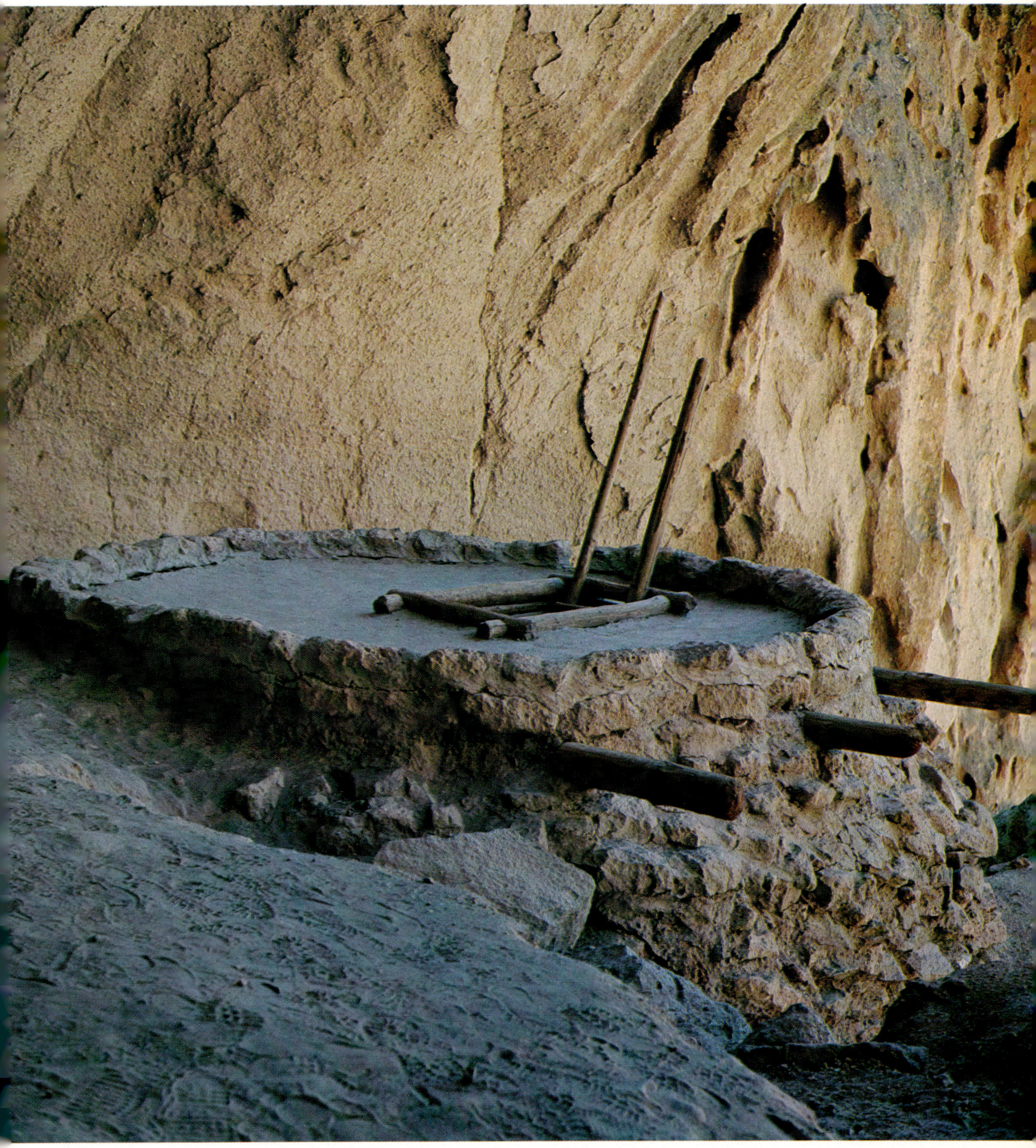

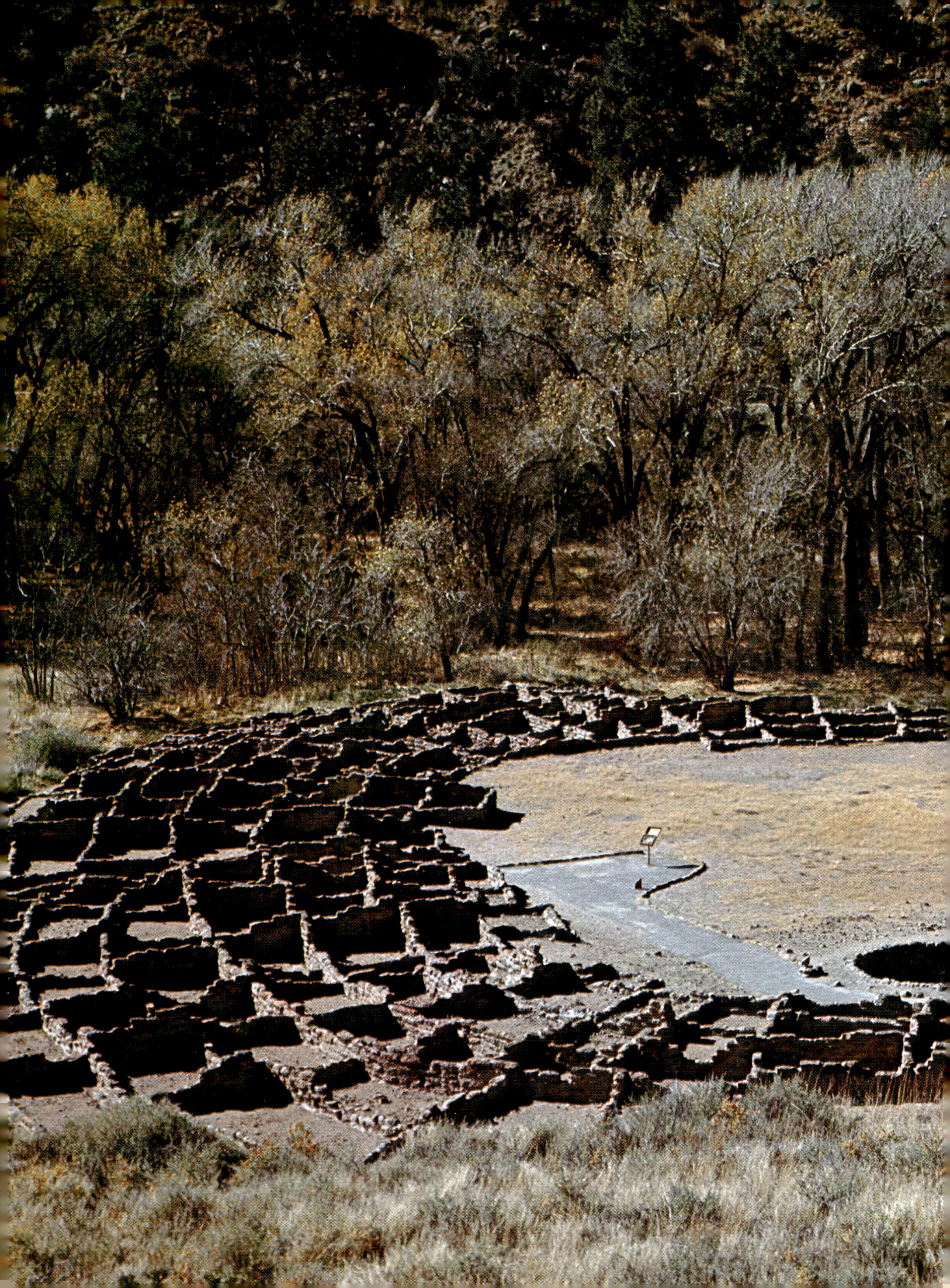

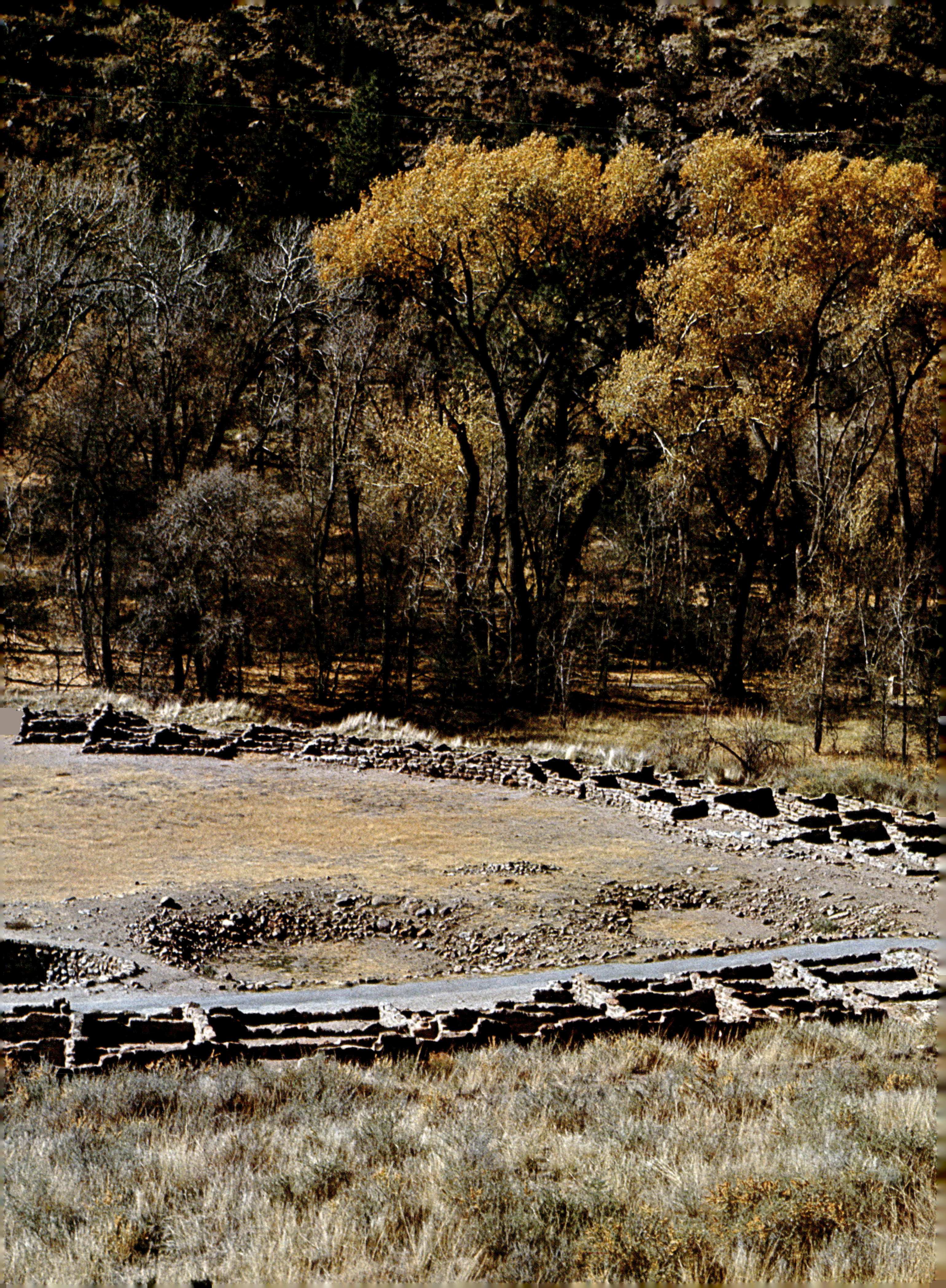

11

12 13

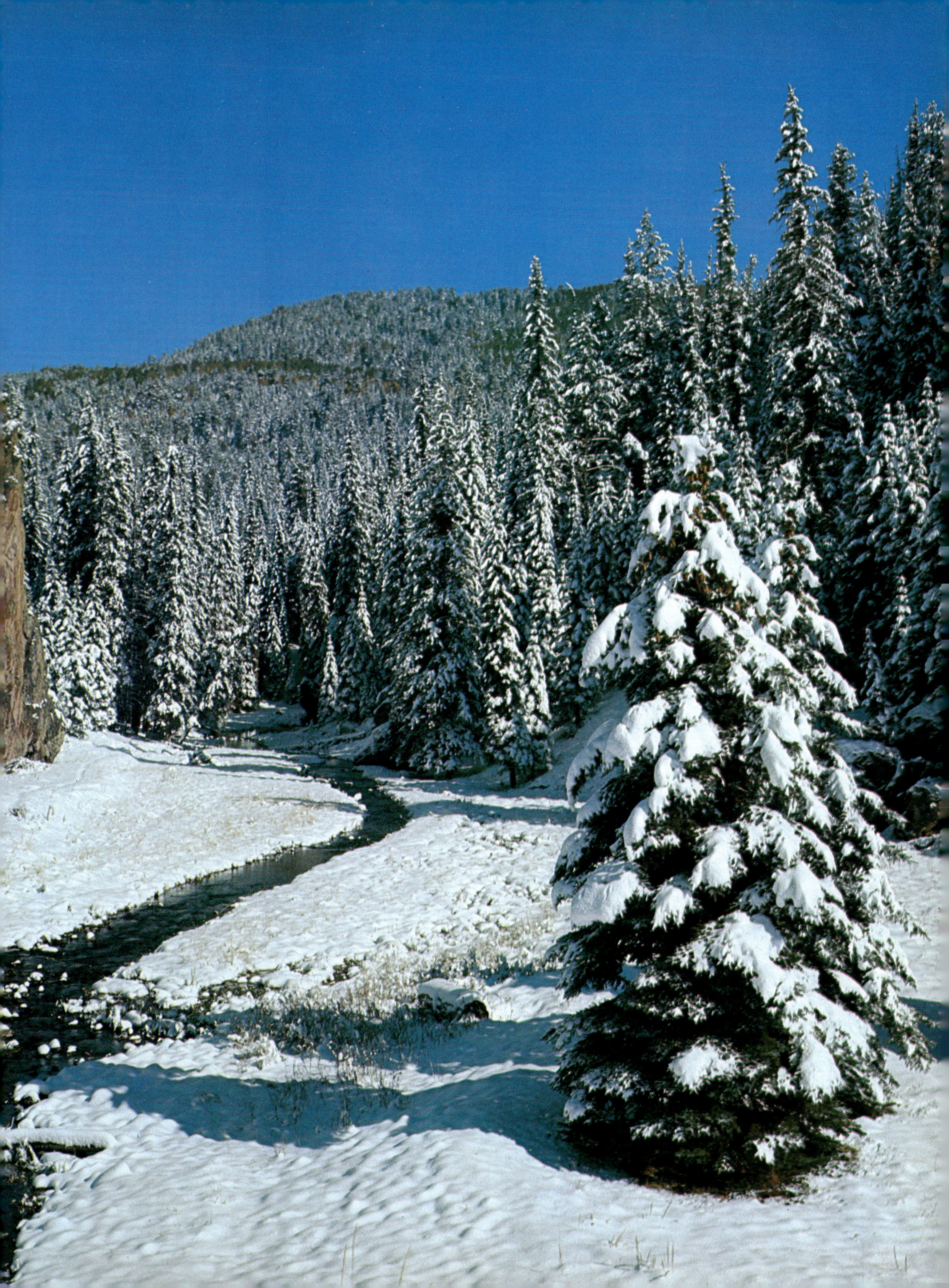

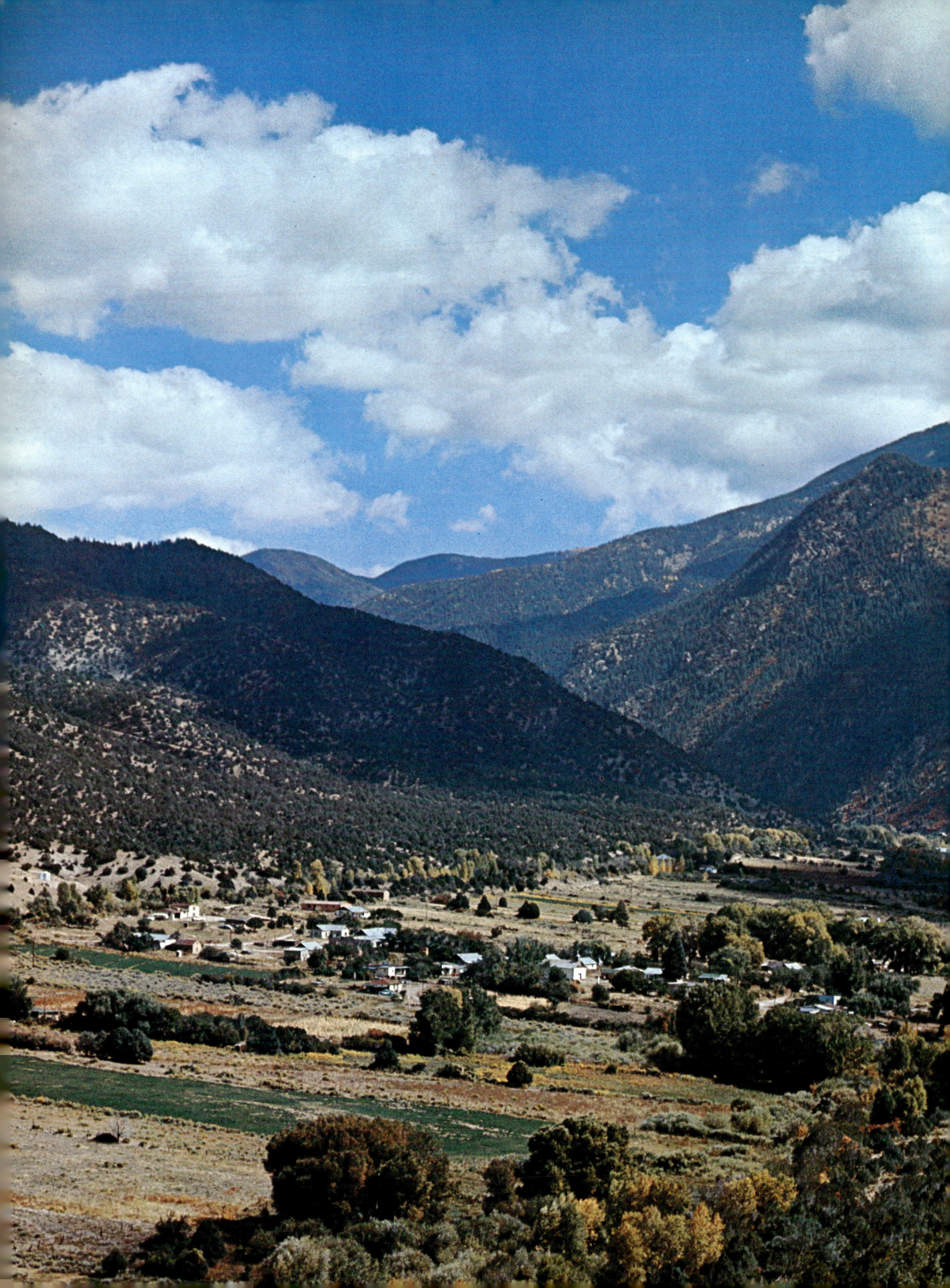

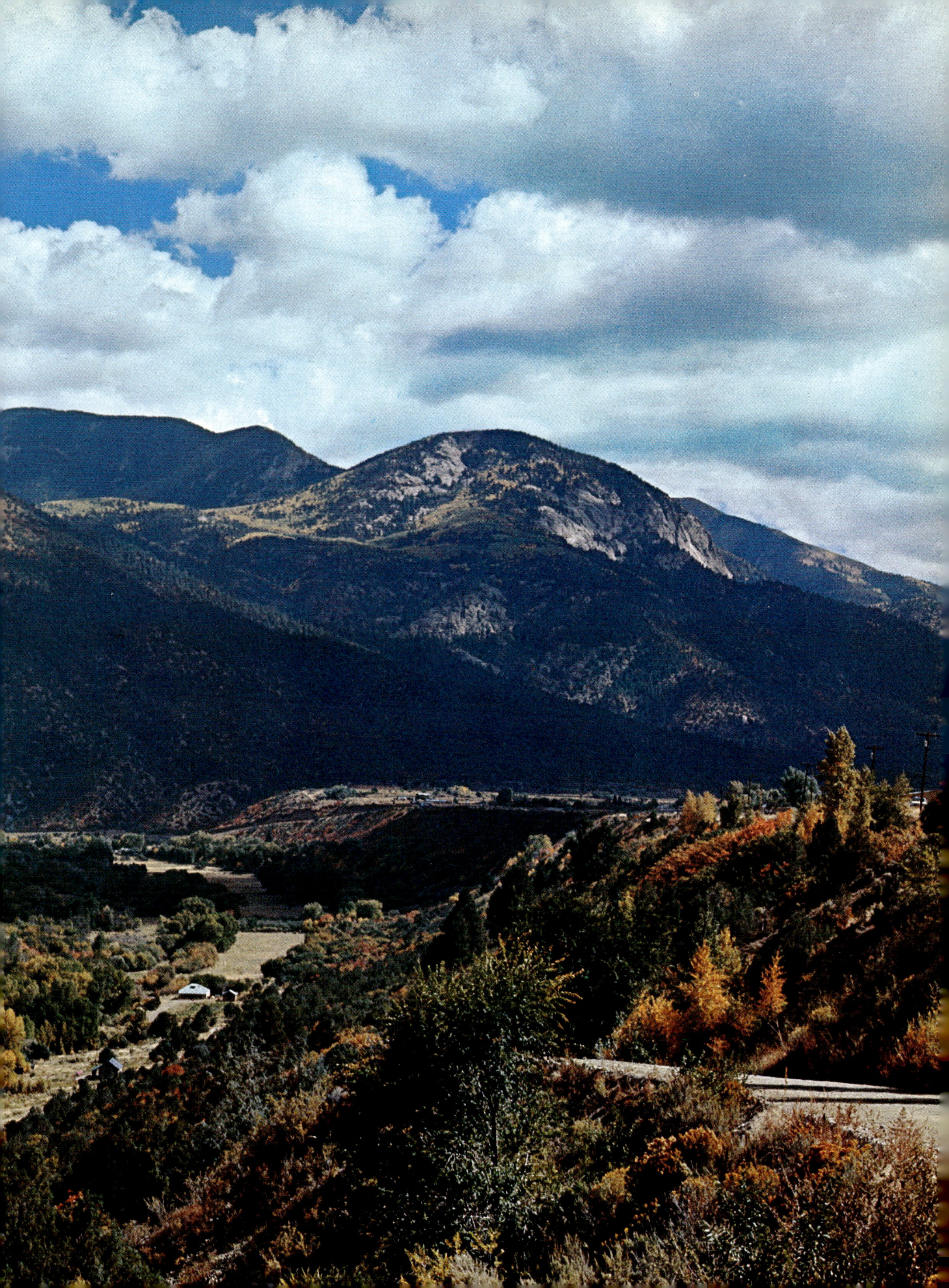

15

16

17

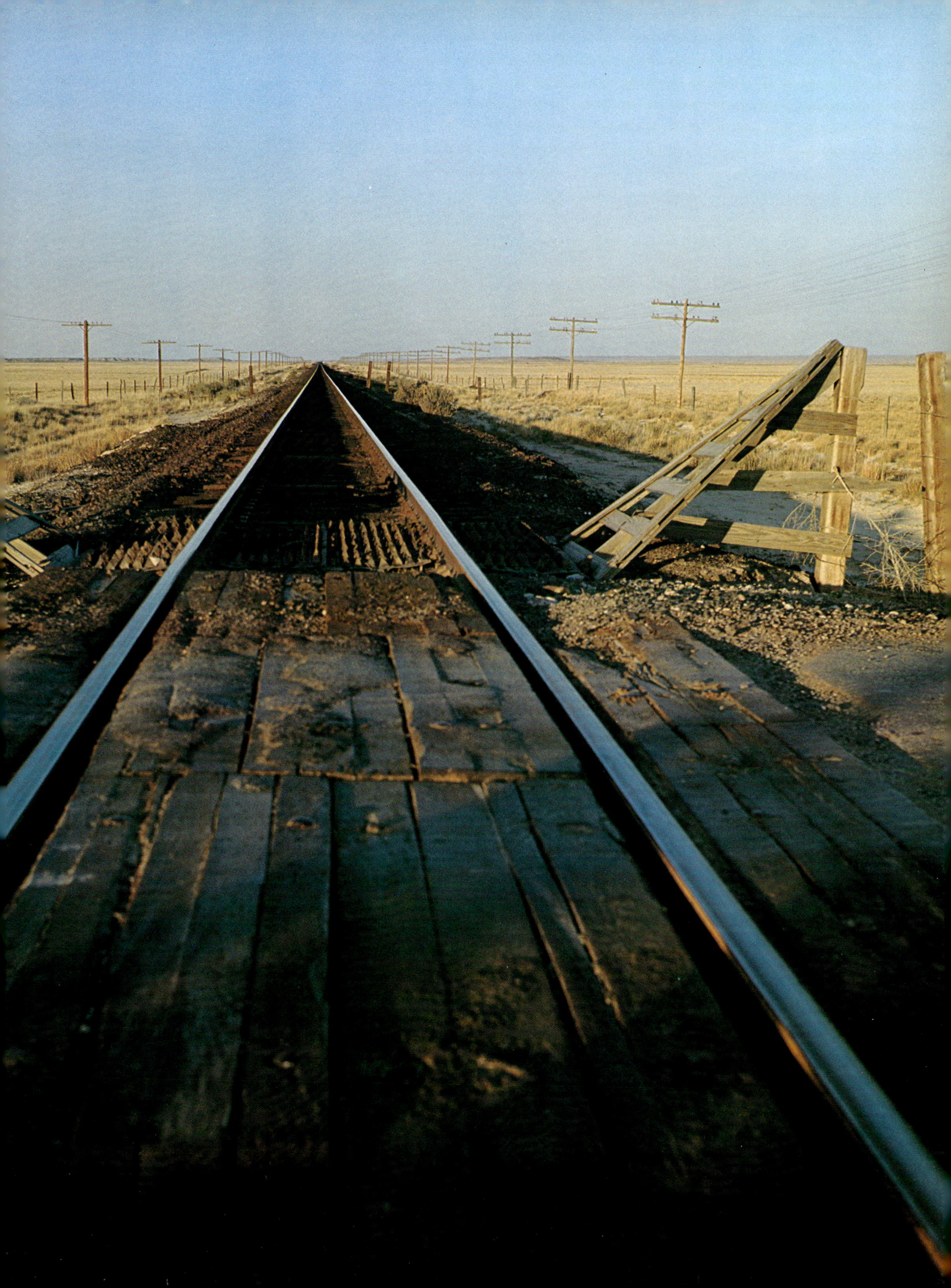

18

19

20
21

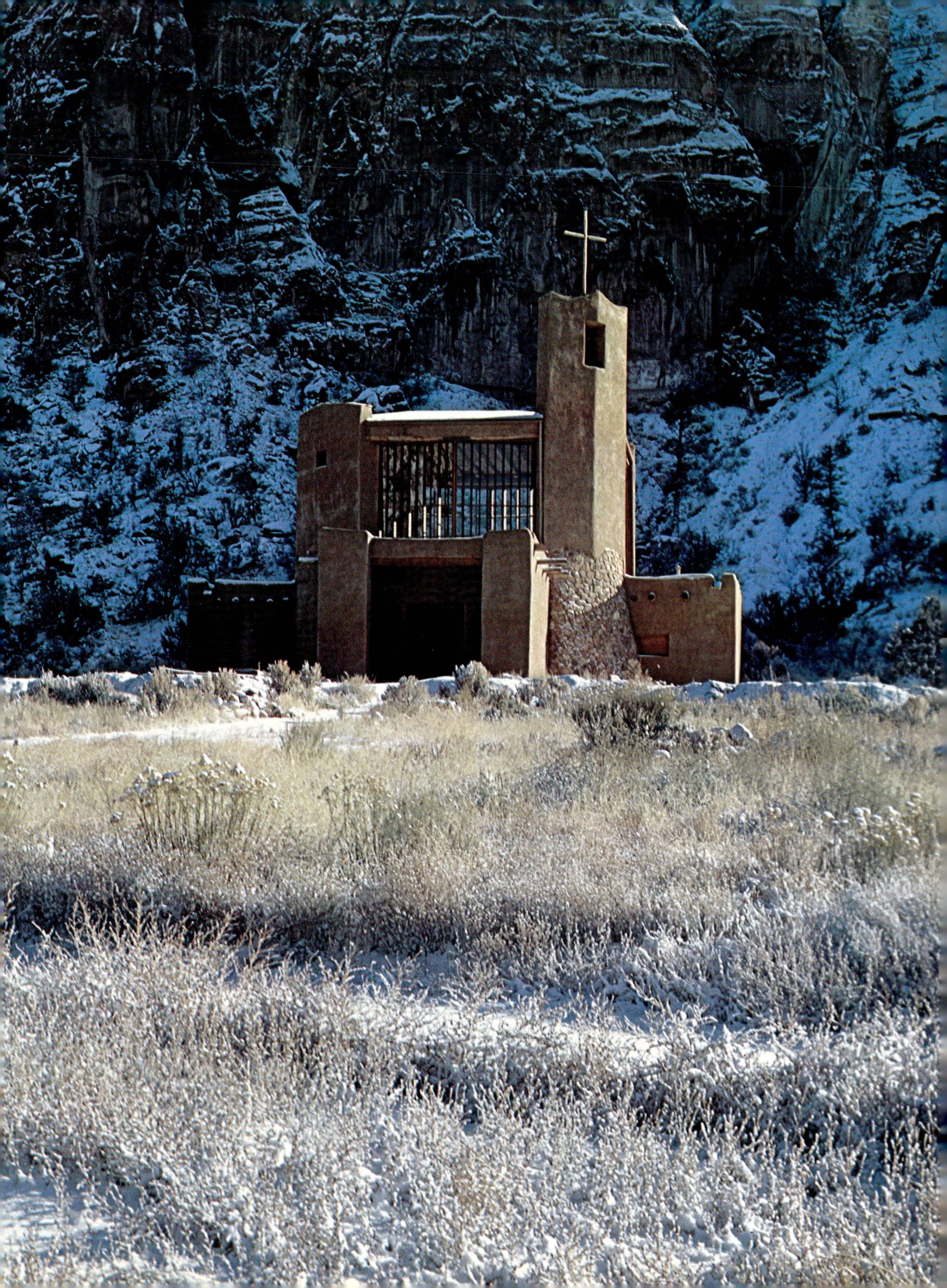

22

23

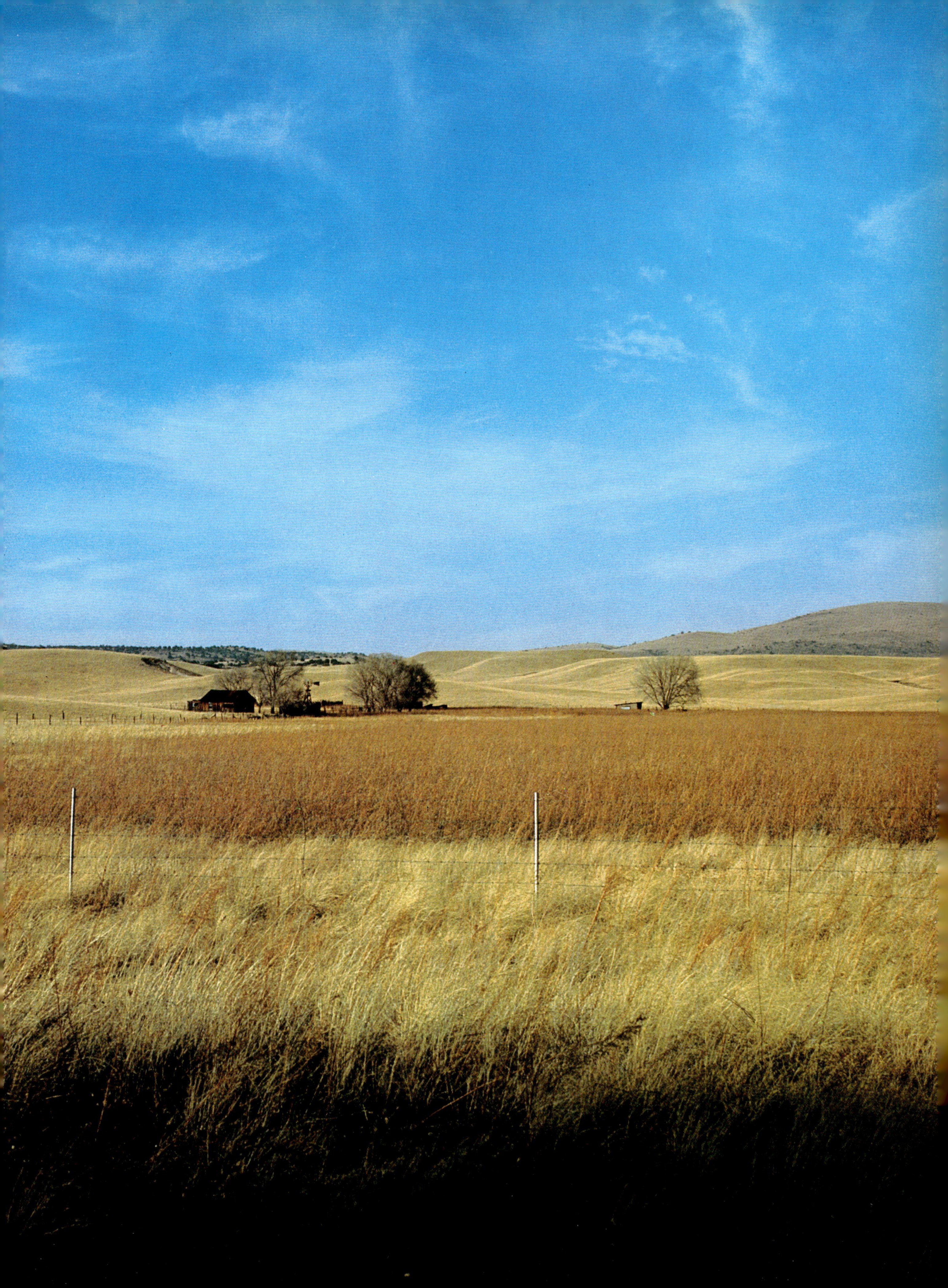

24

25

26

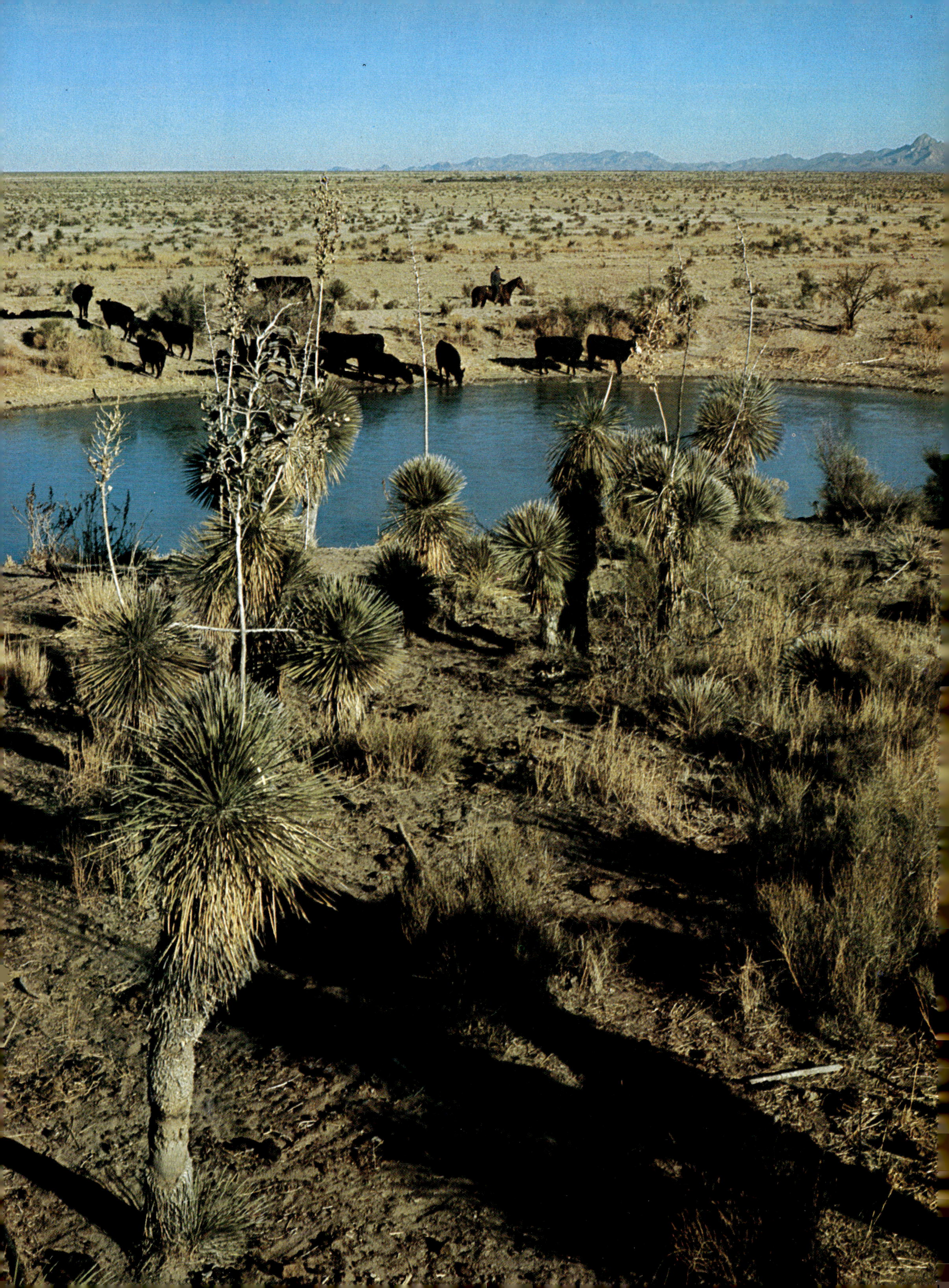

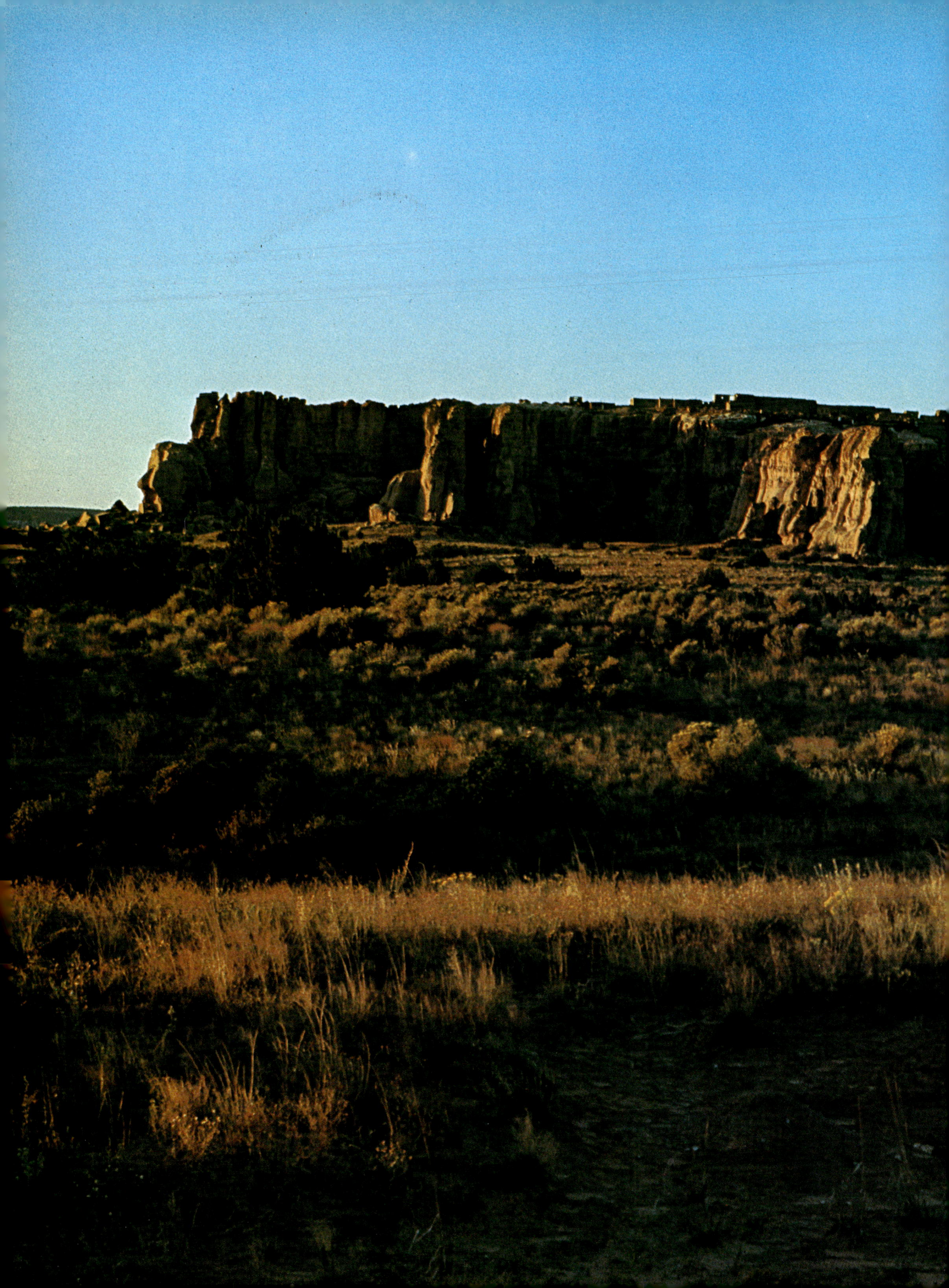

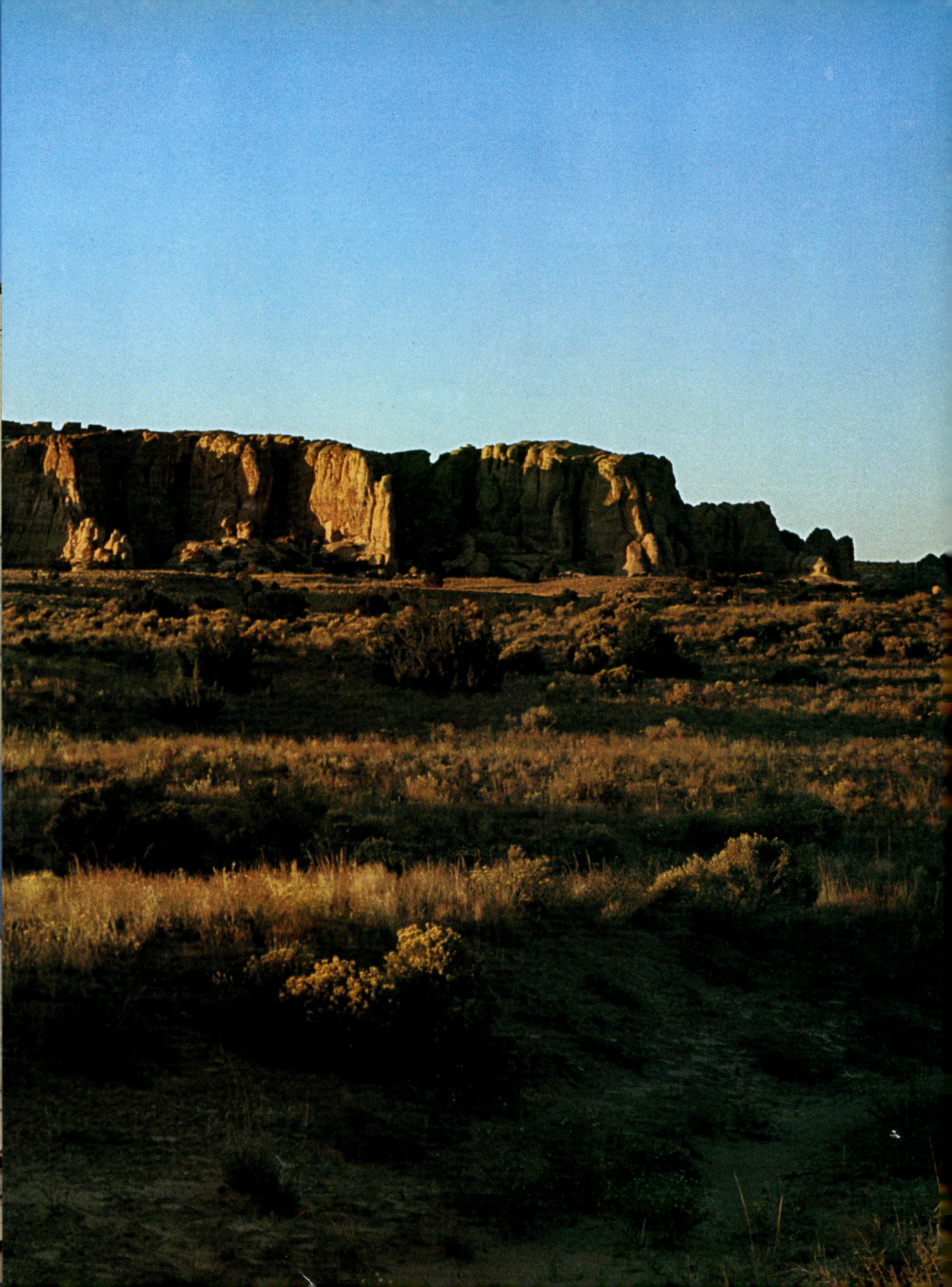

30
31
32

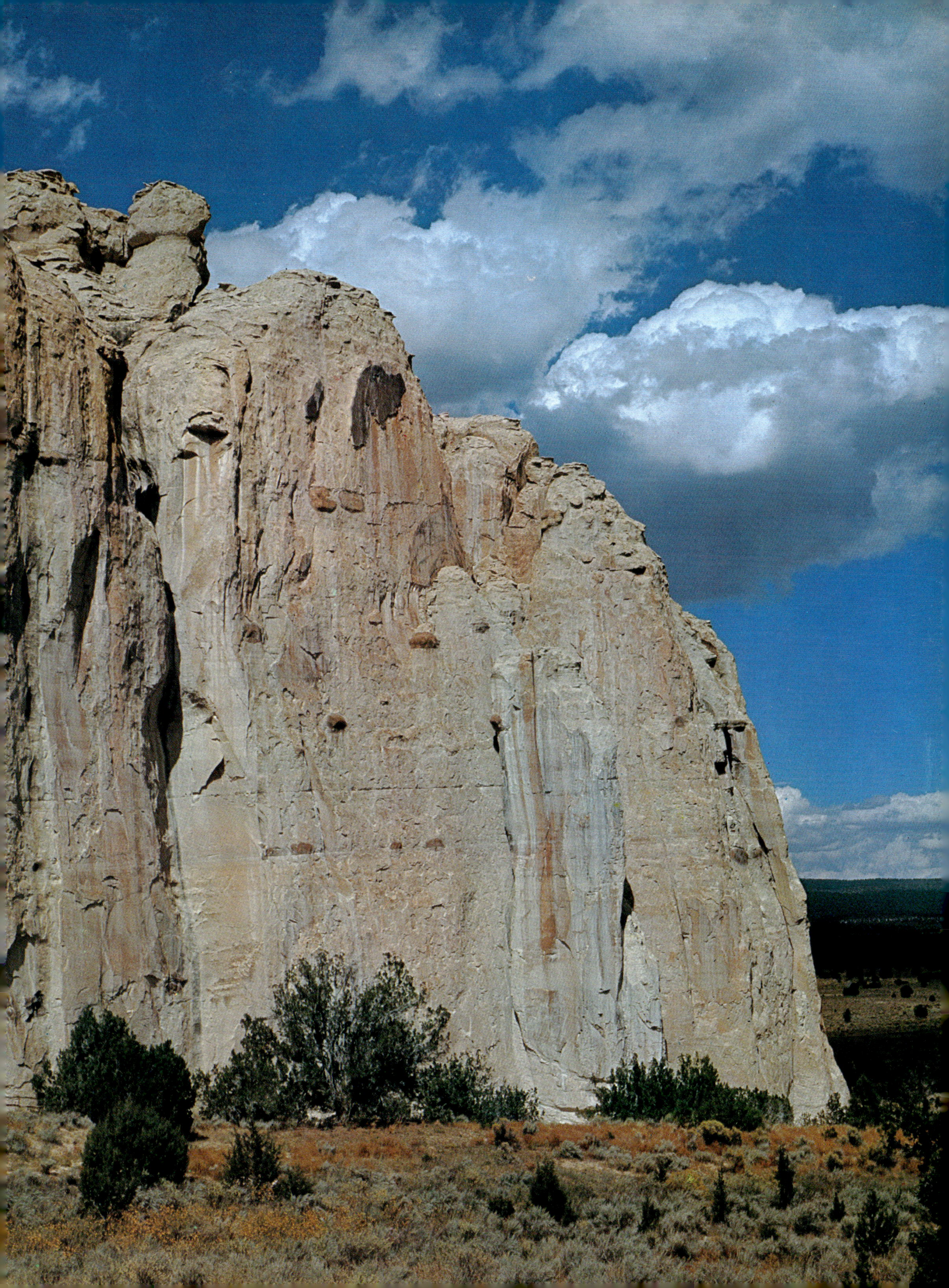

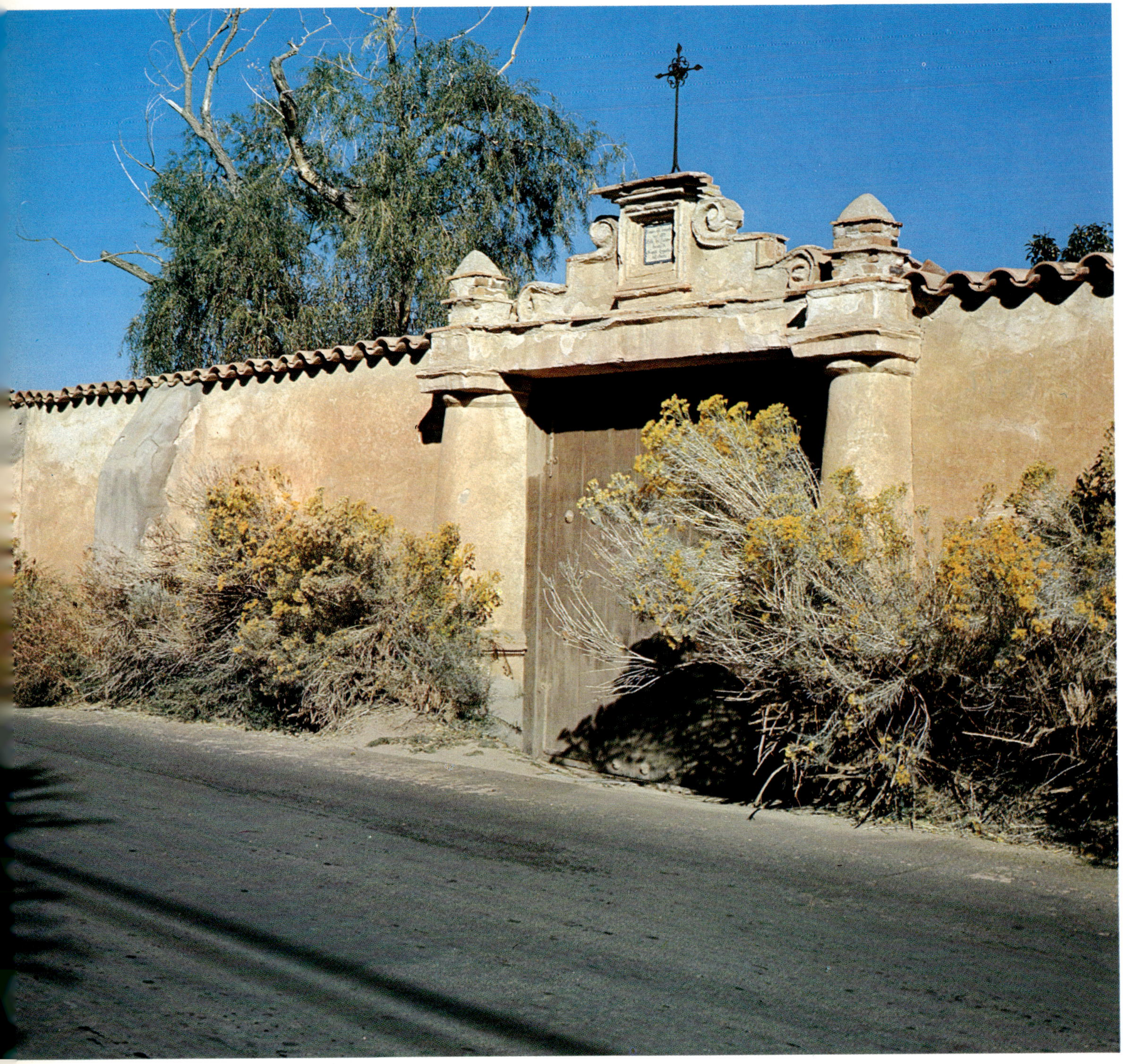

33

34

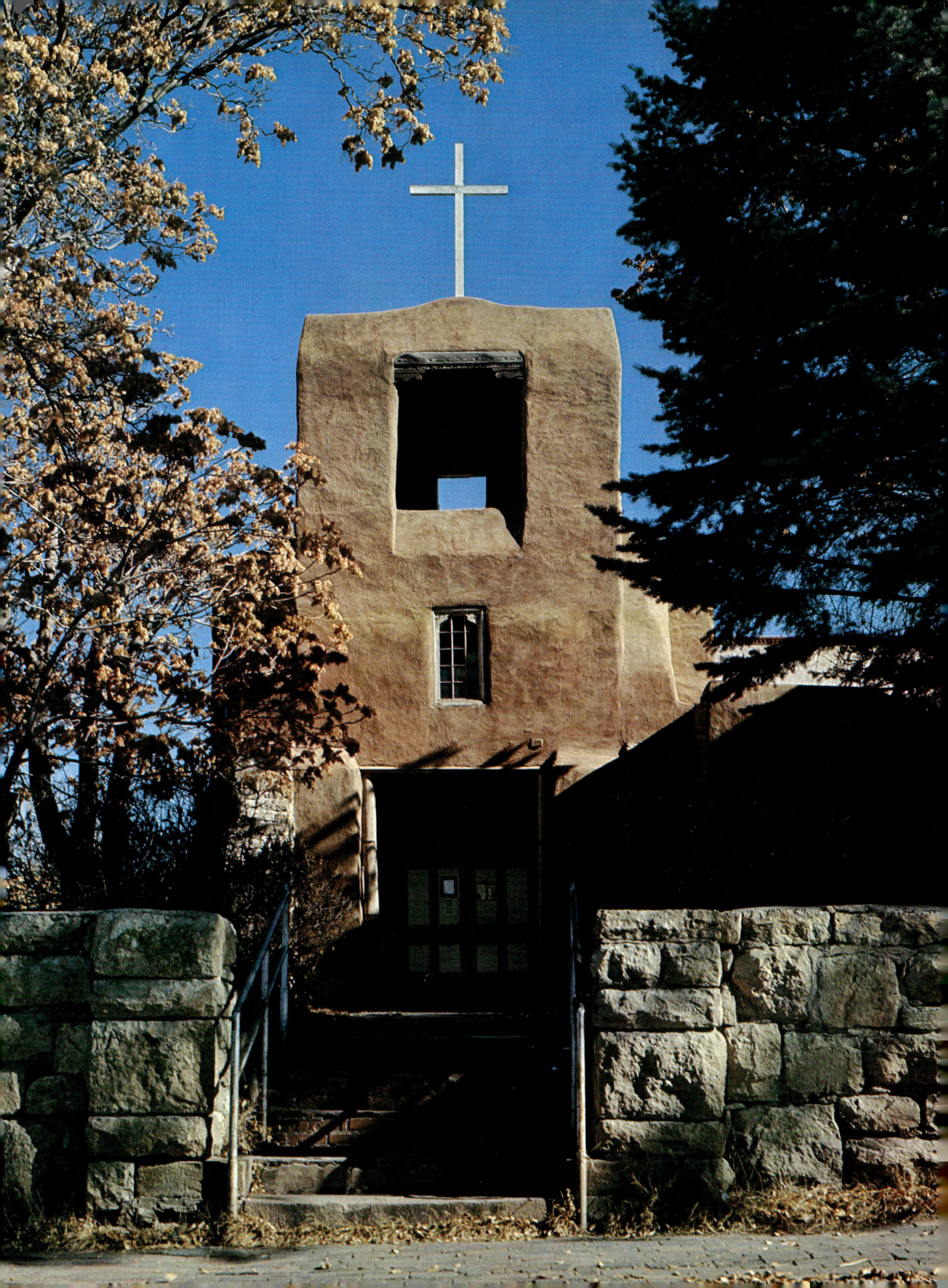

35

36

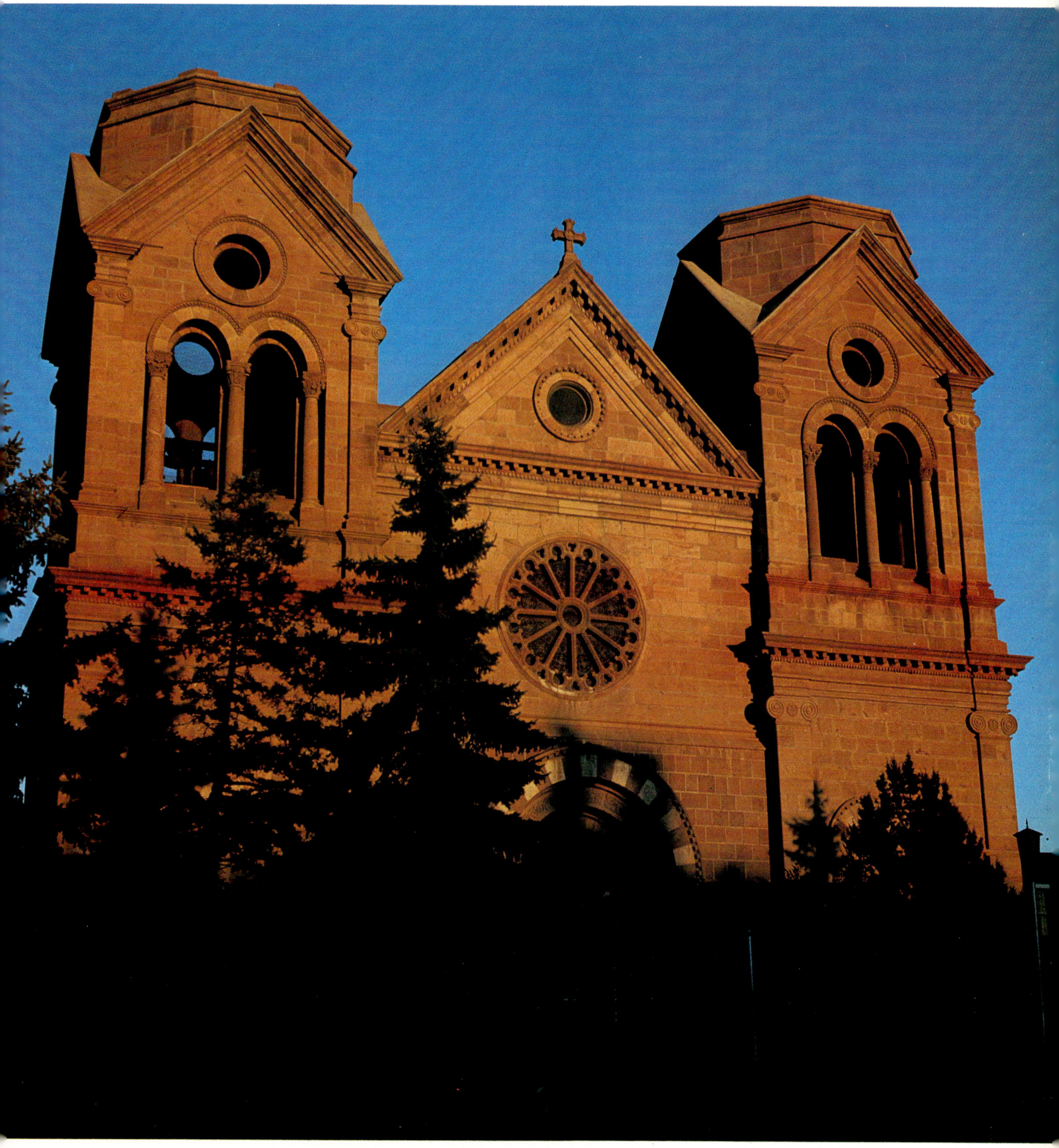

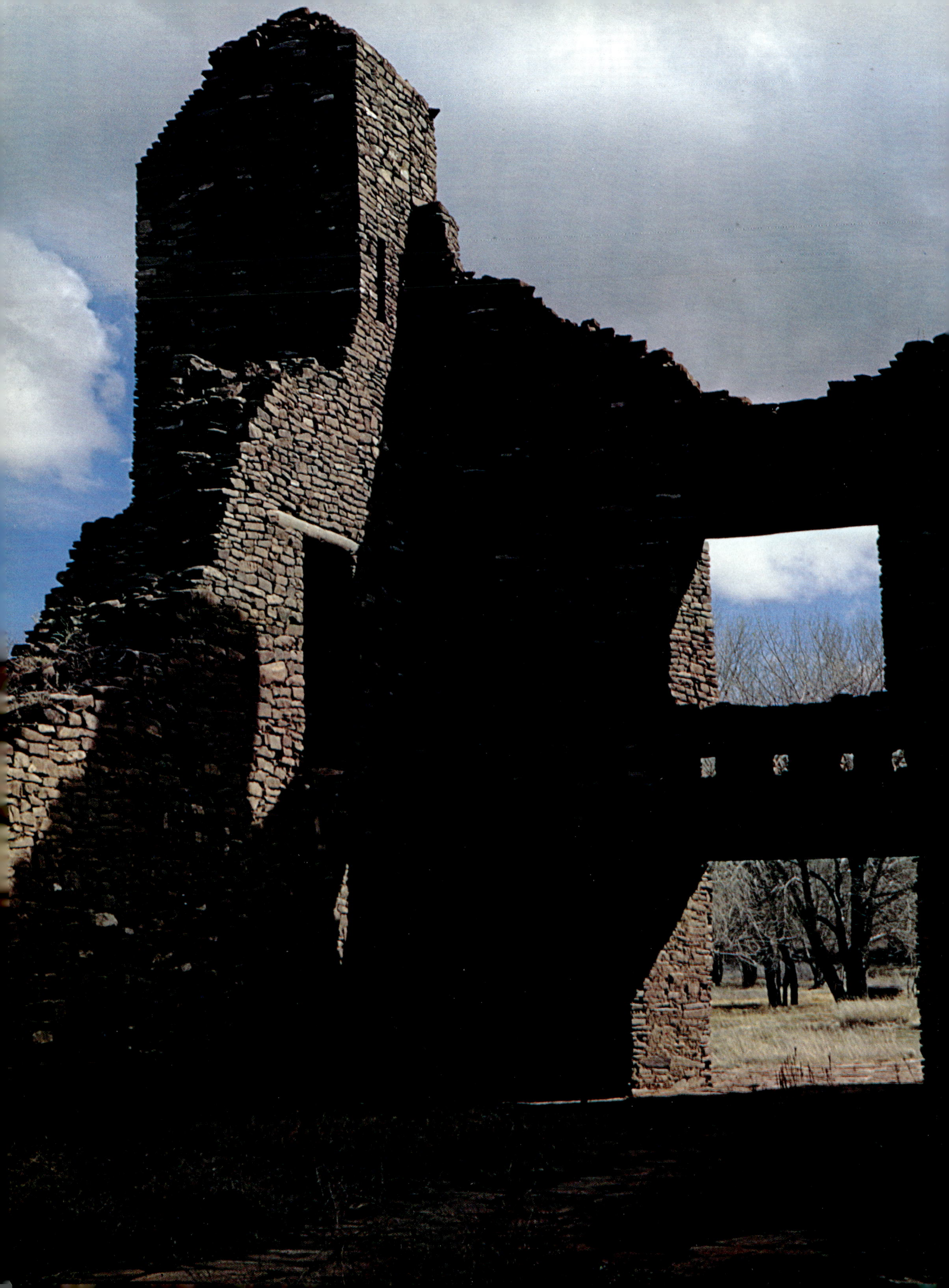

39

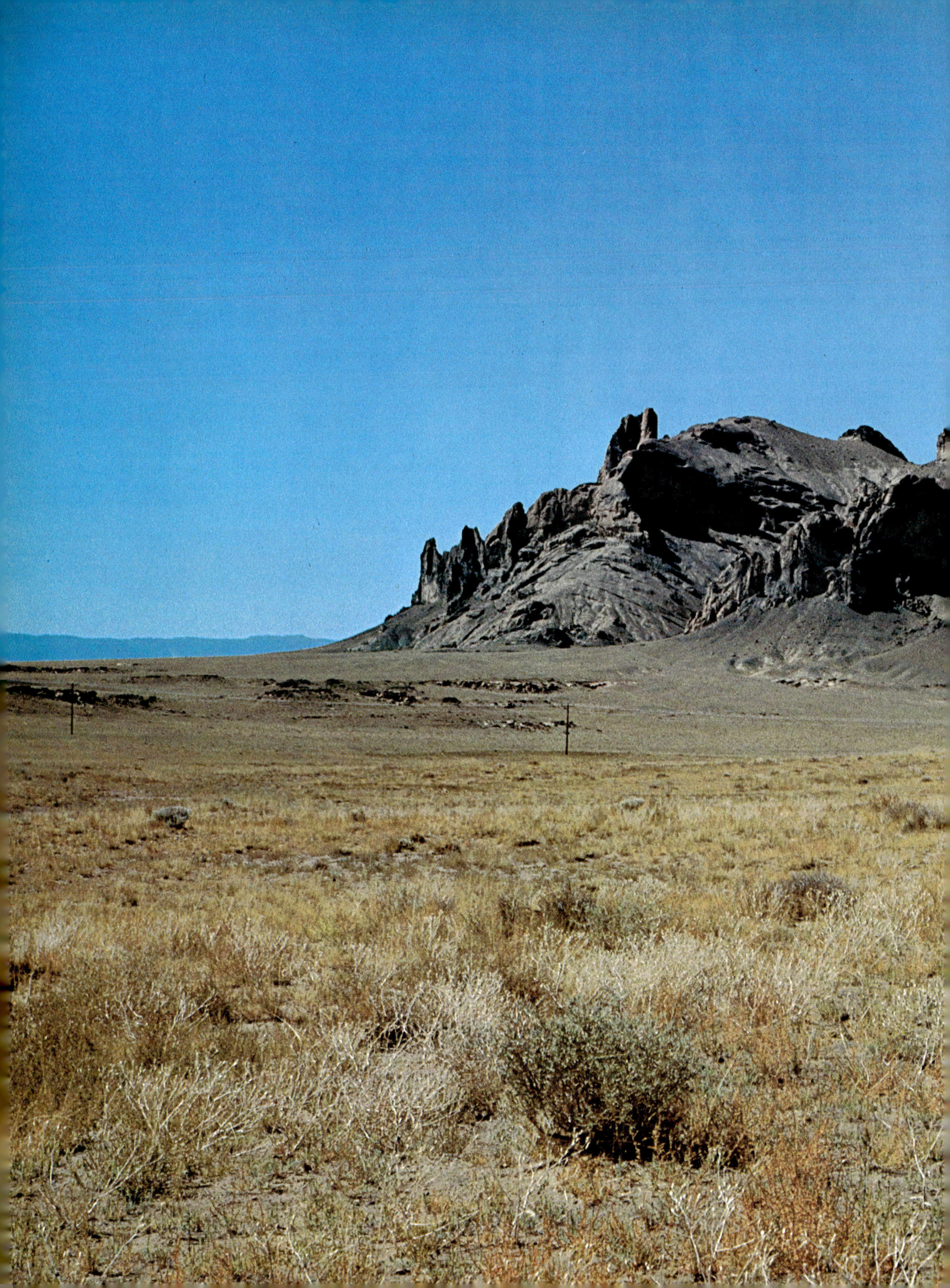

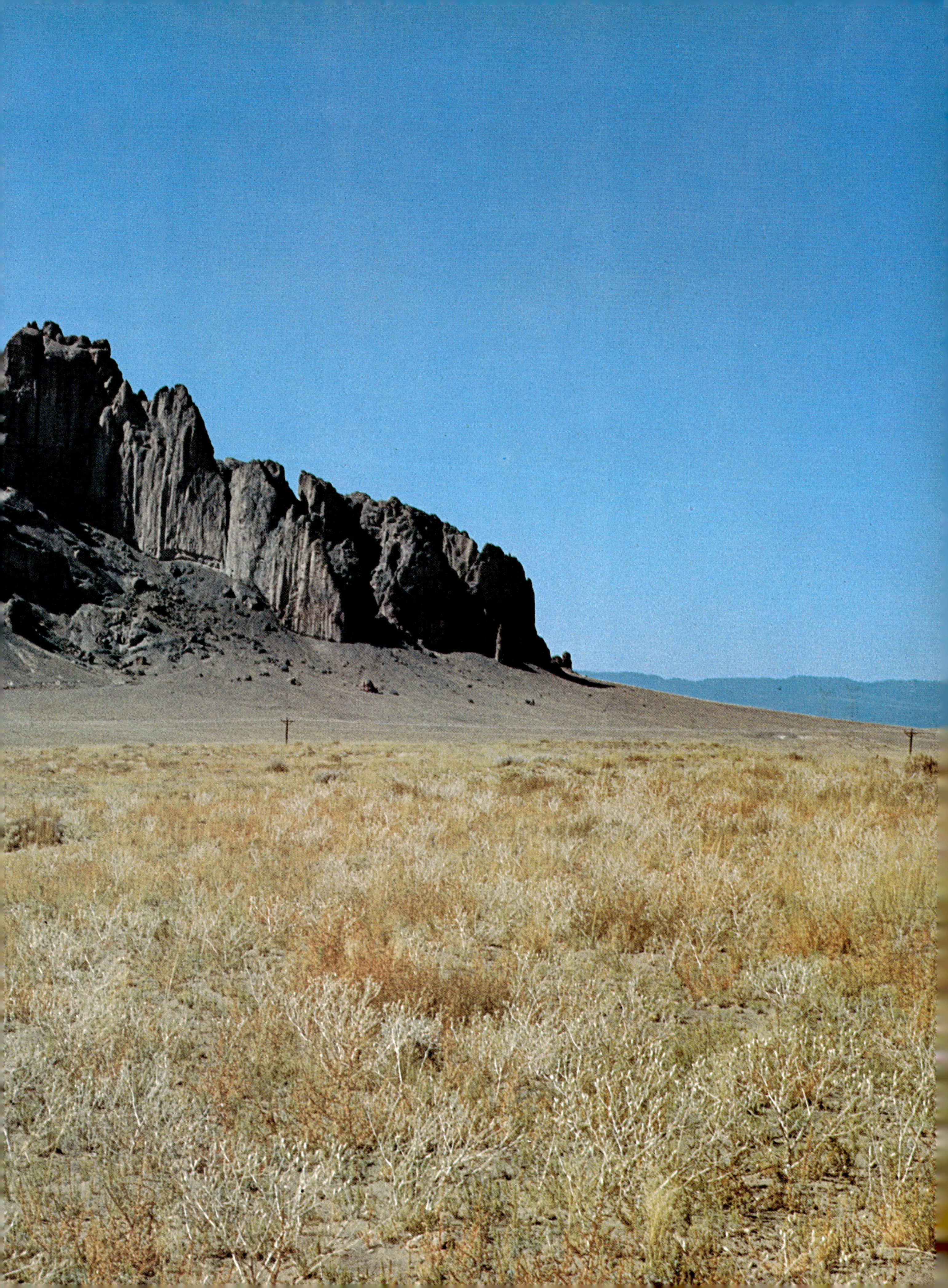

41

42

43

44

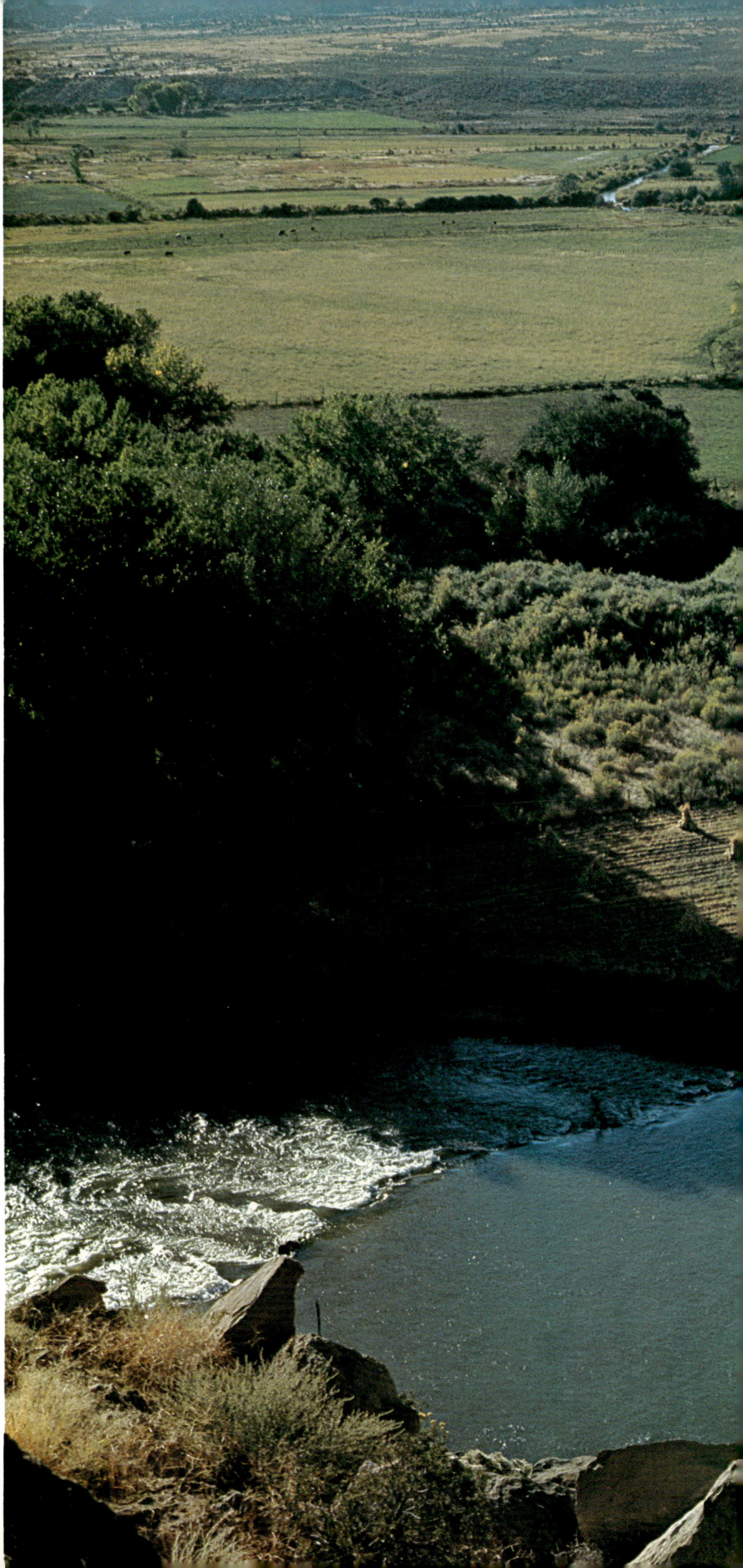

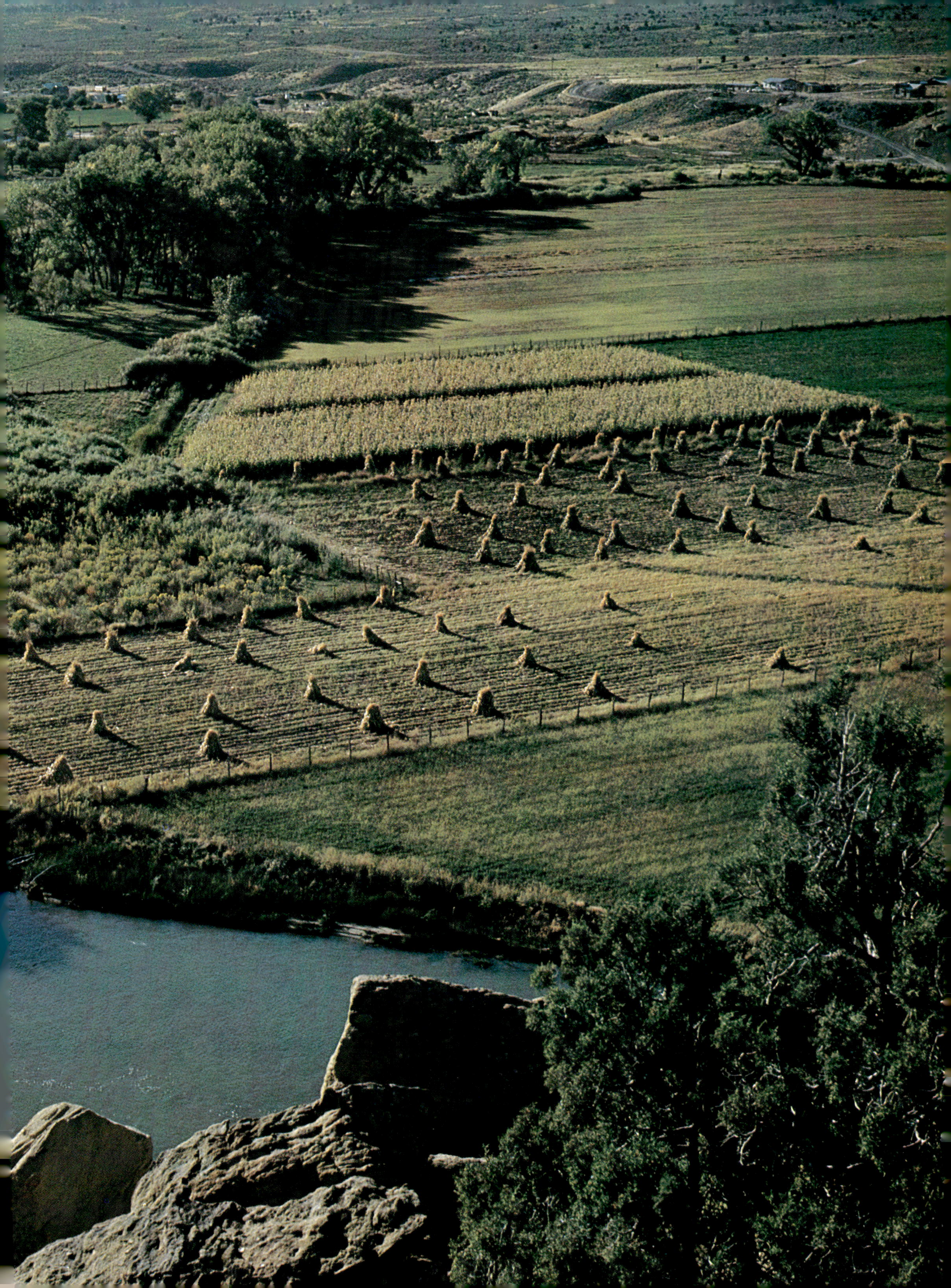

46

47

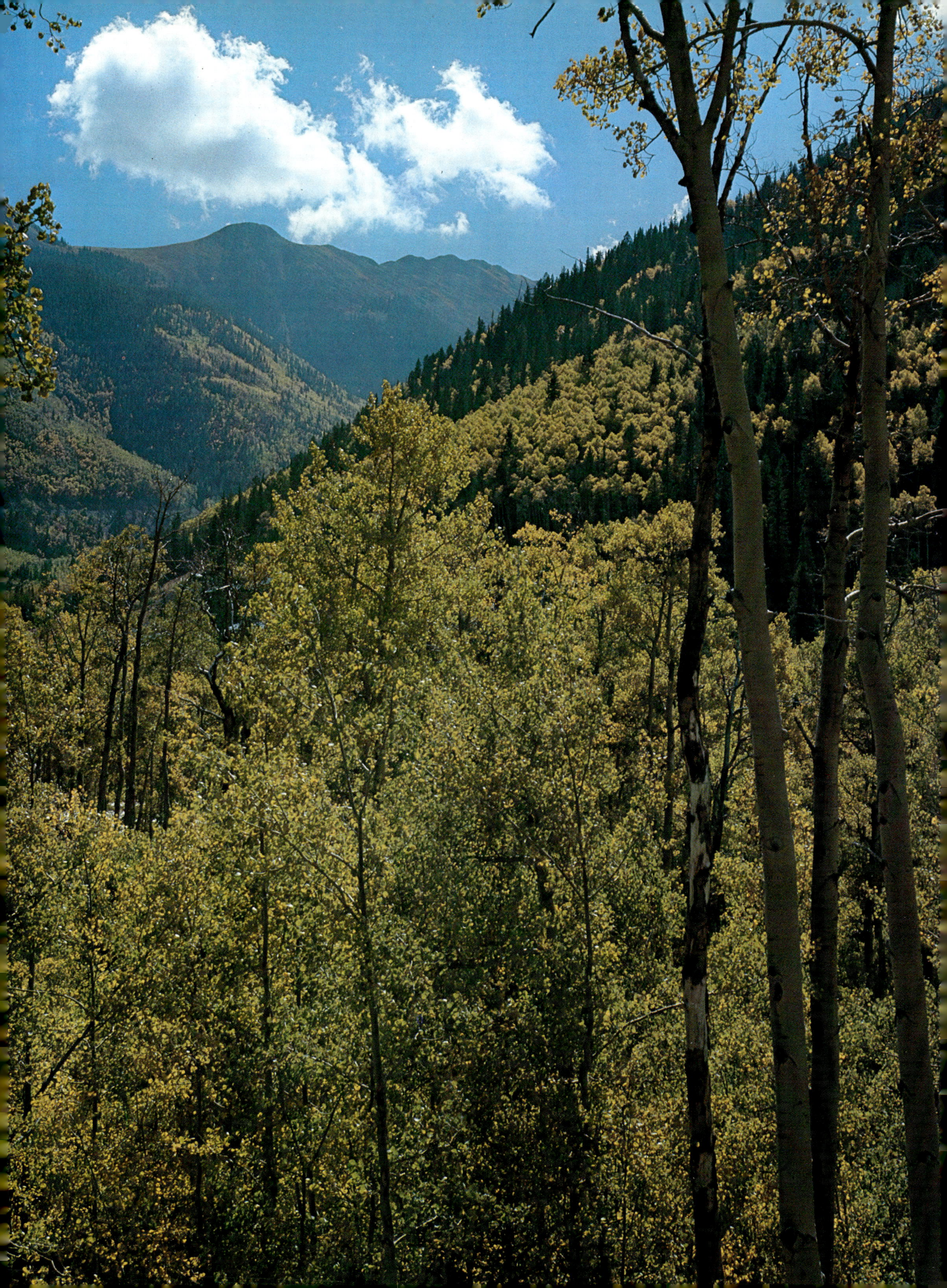

48

49

50

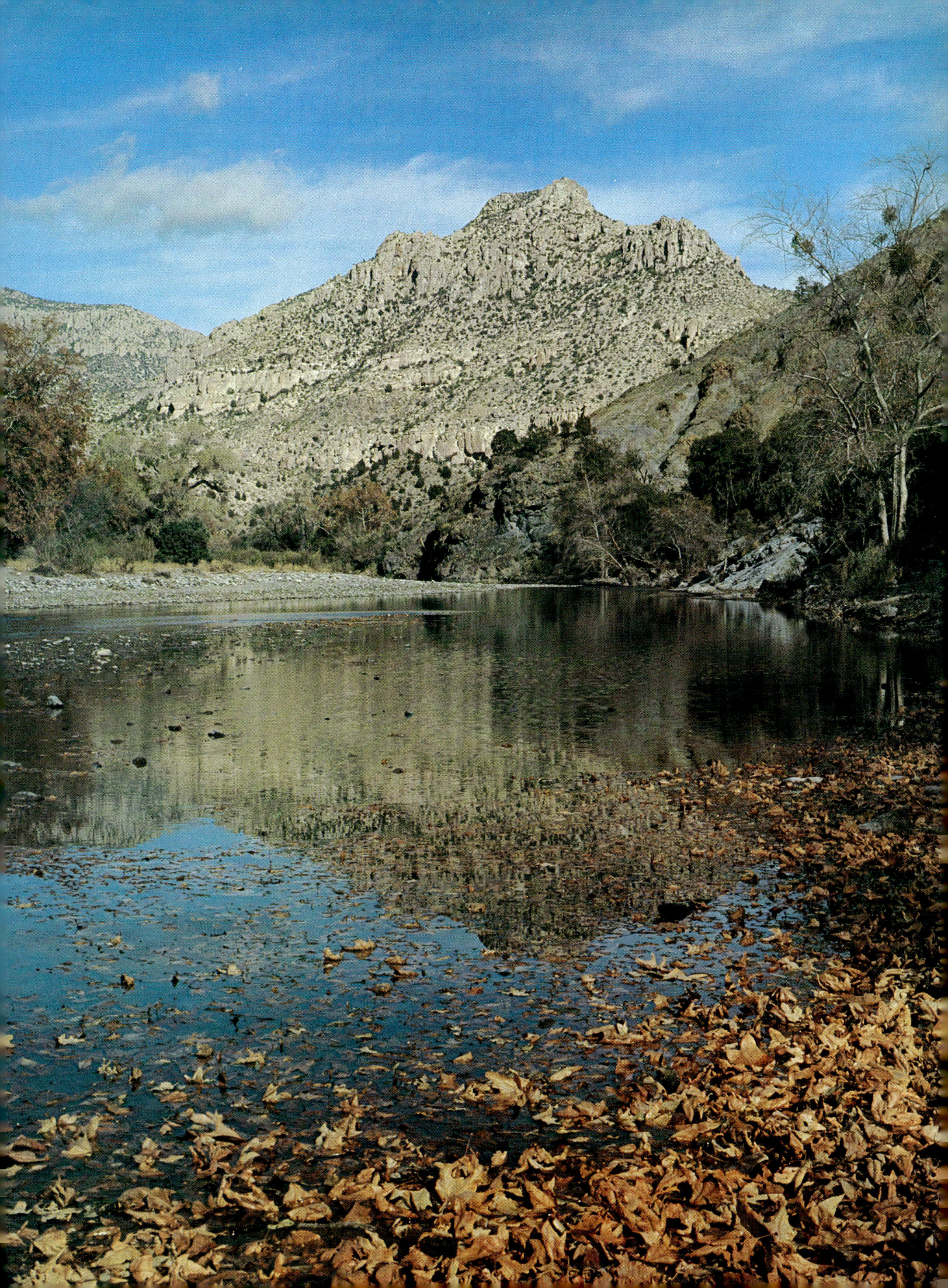

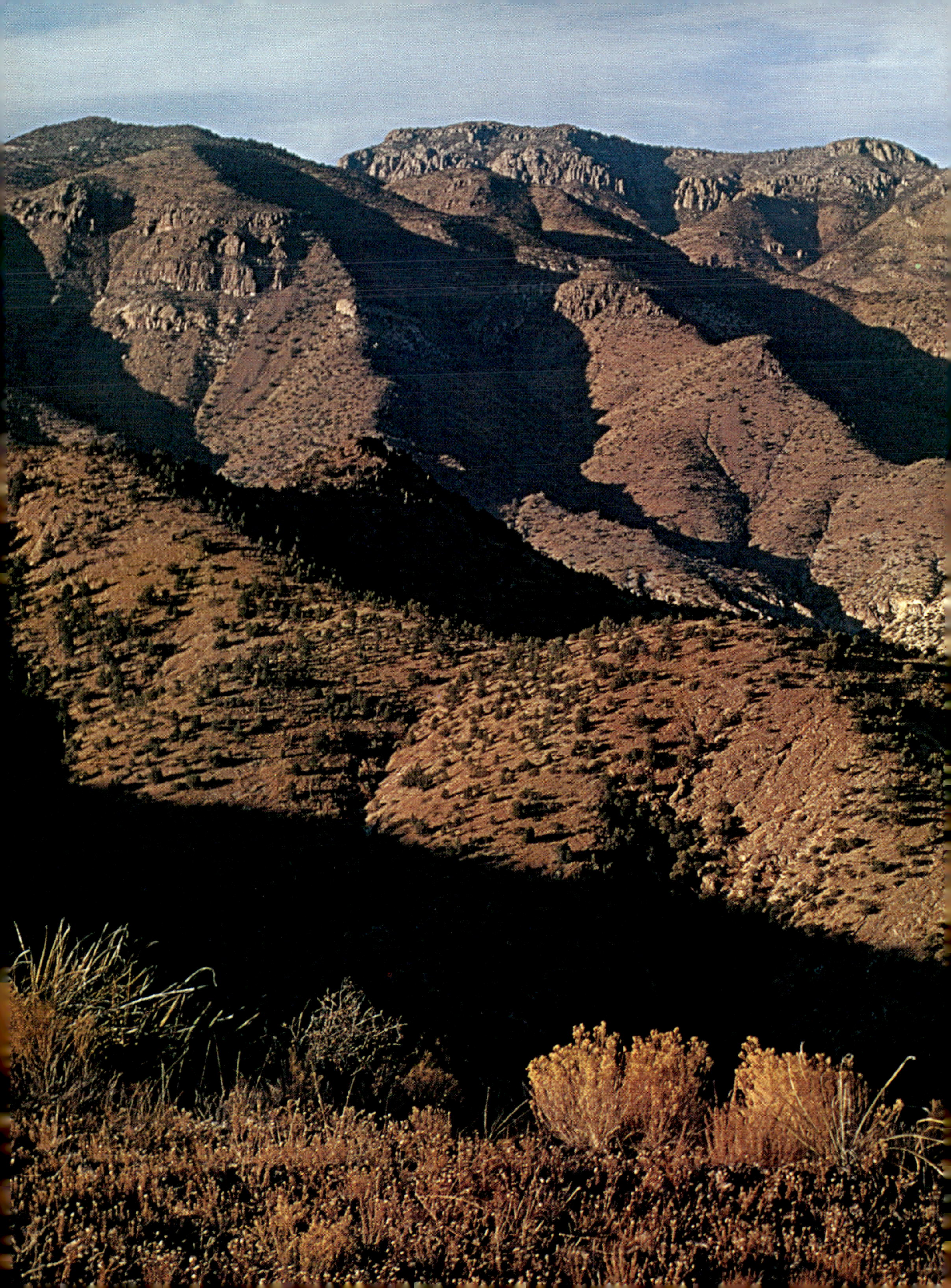

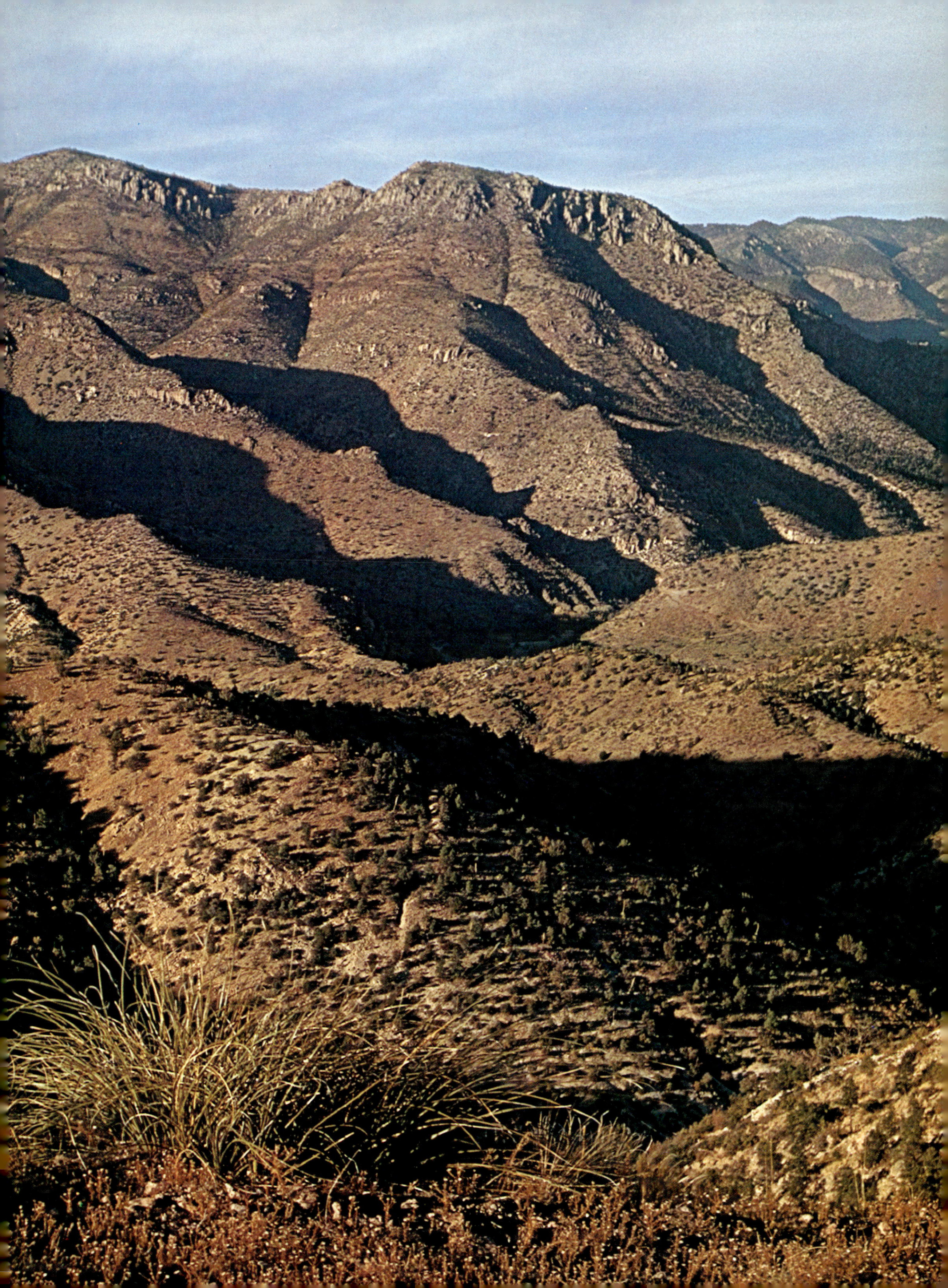

52

53

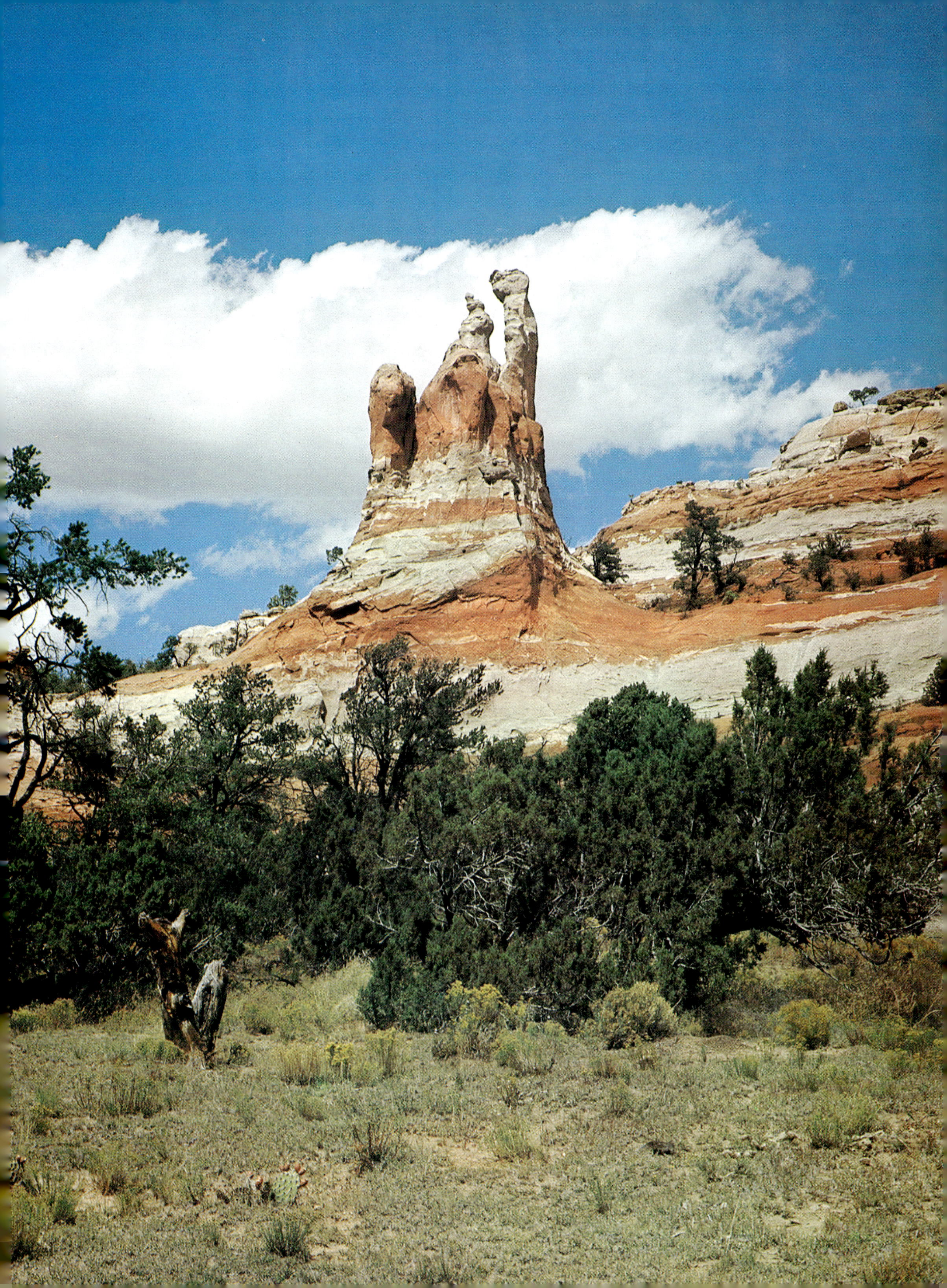

54

55

56

57 ▶

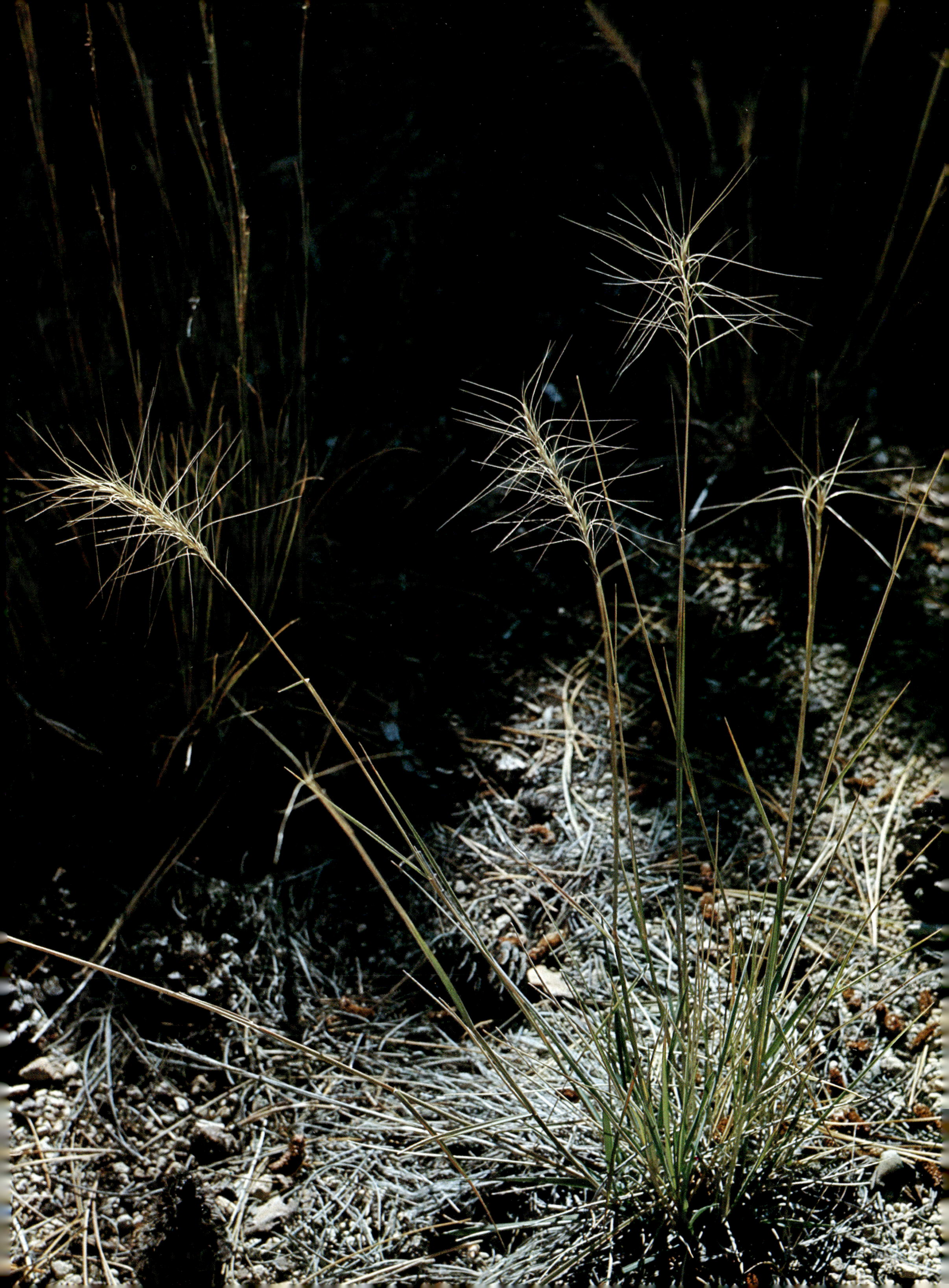

58

59

60

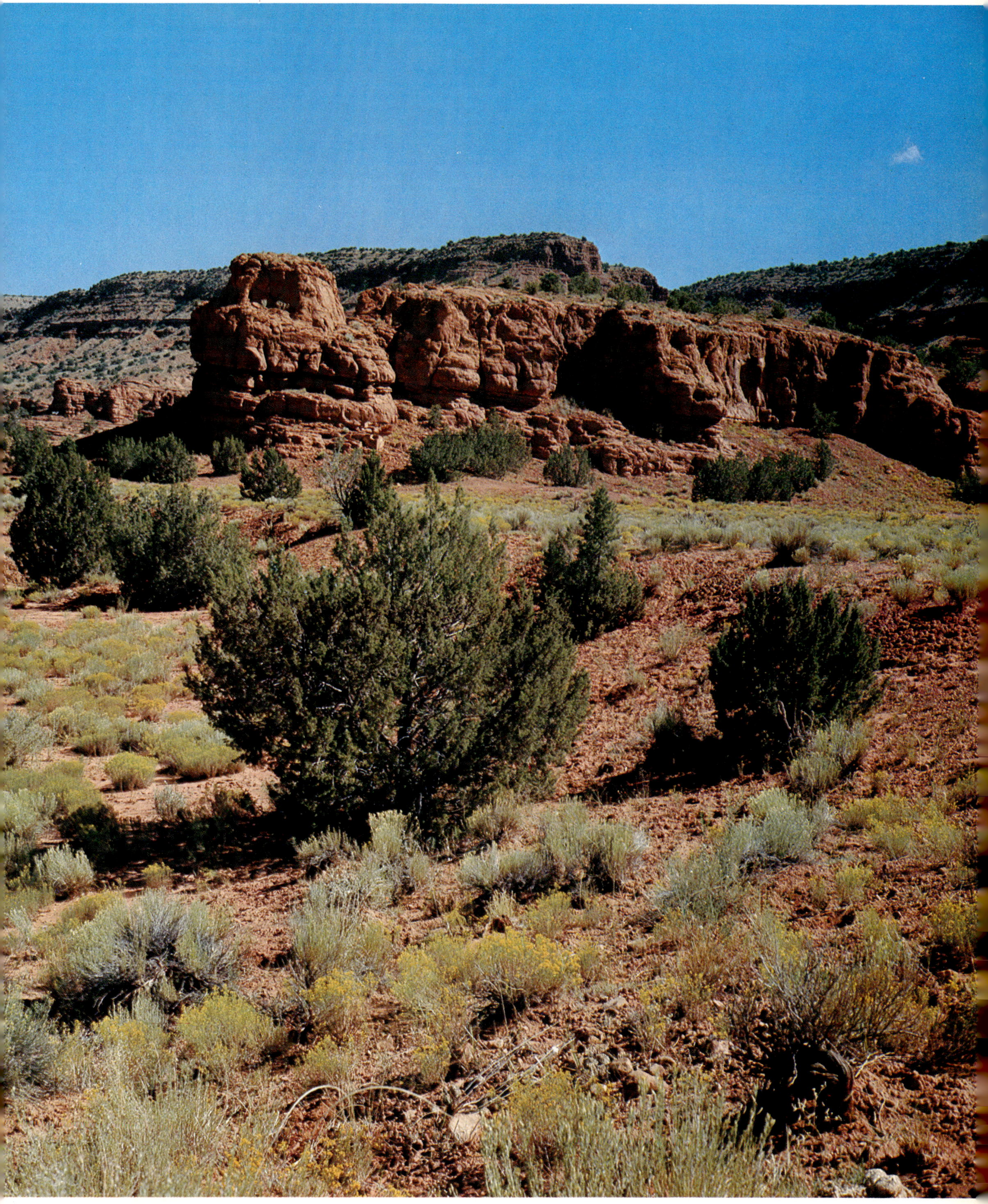

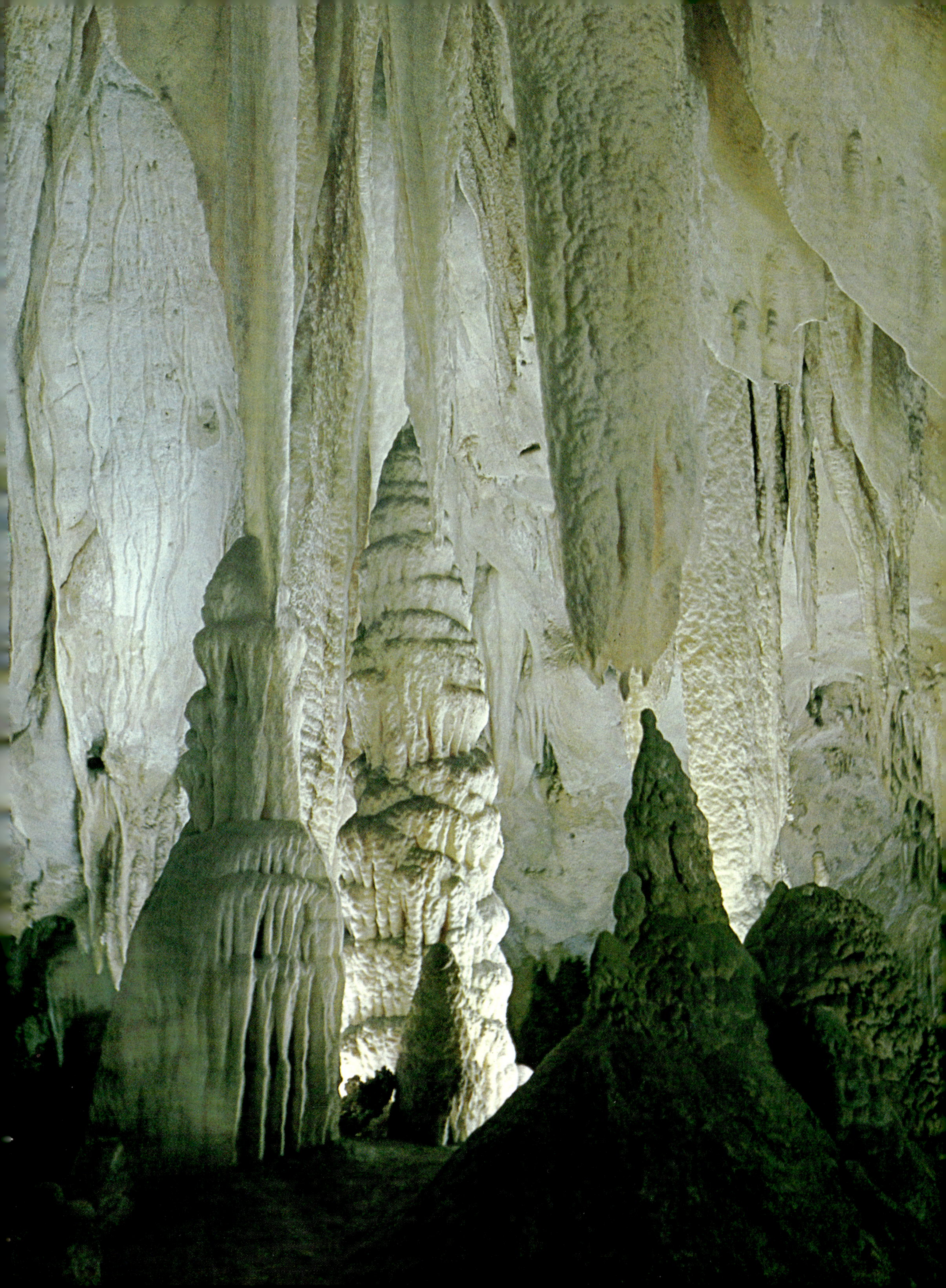

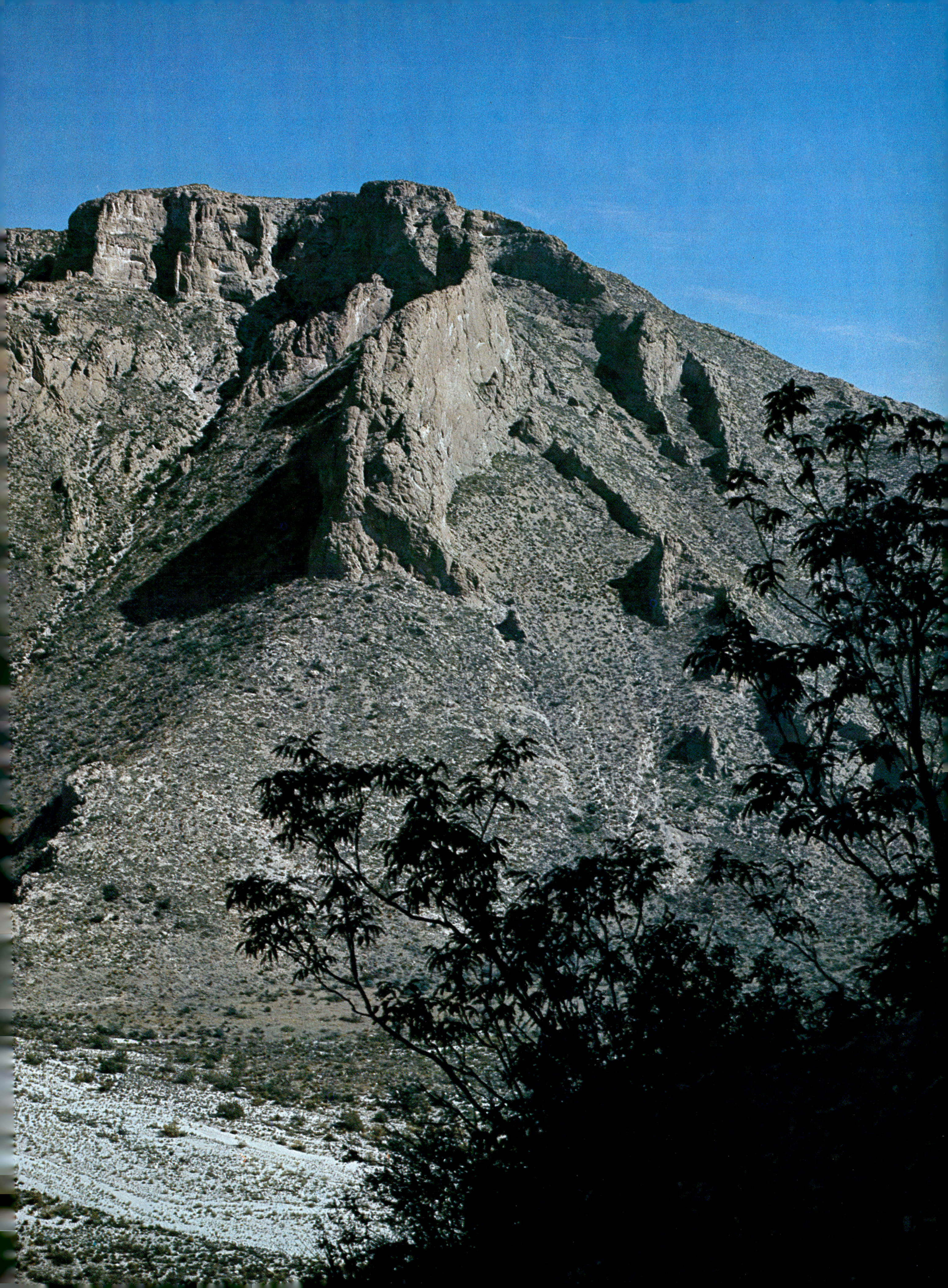

63

64

65

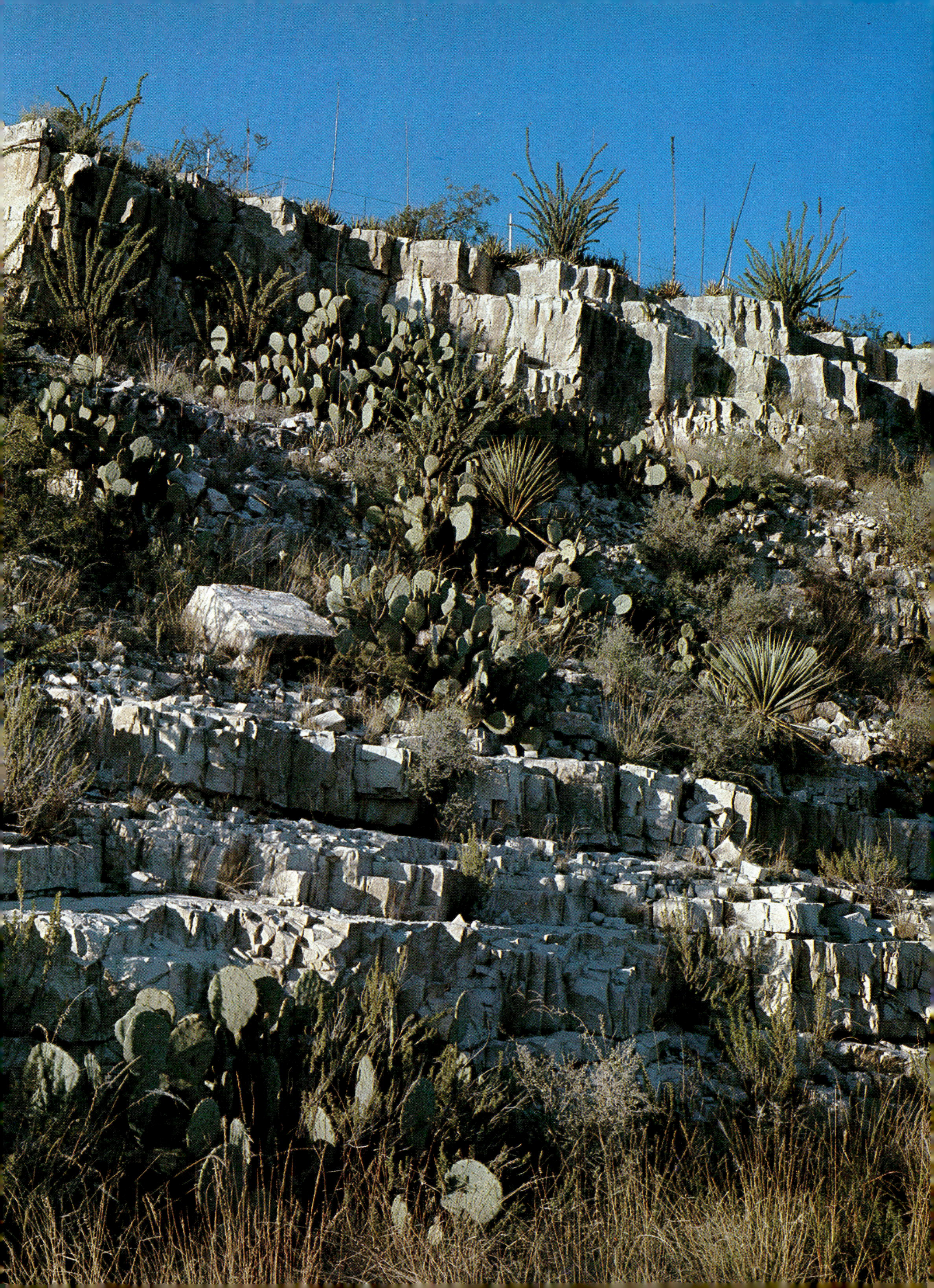

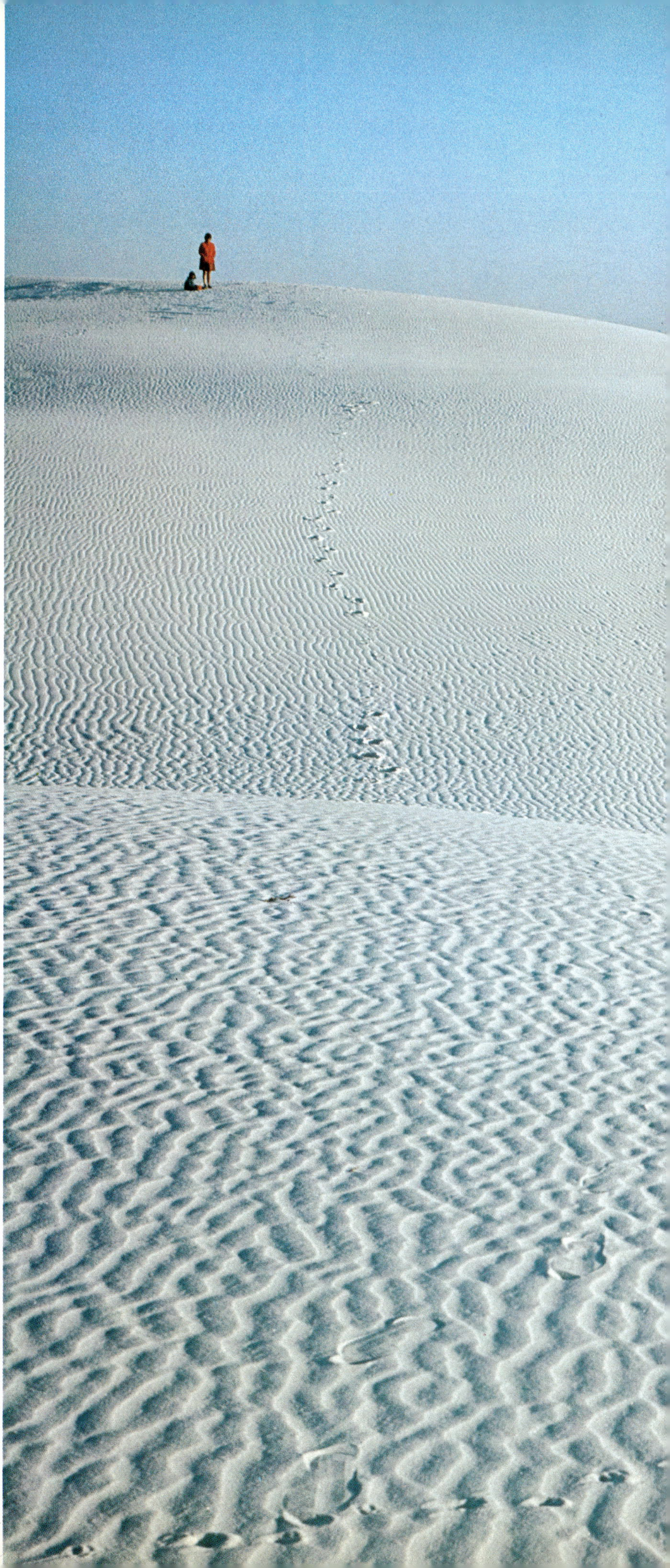

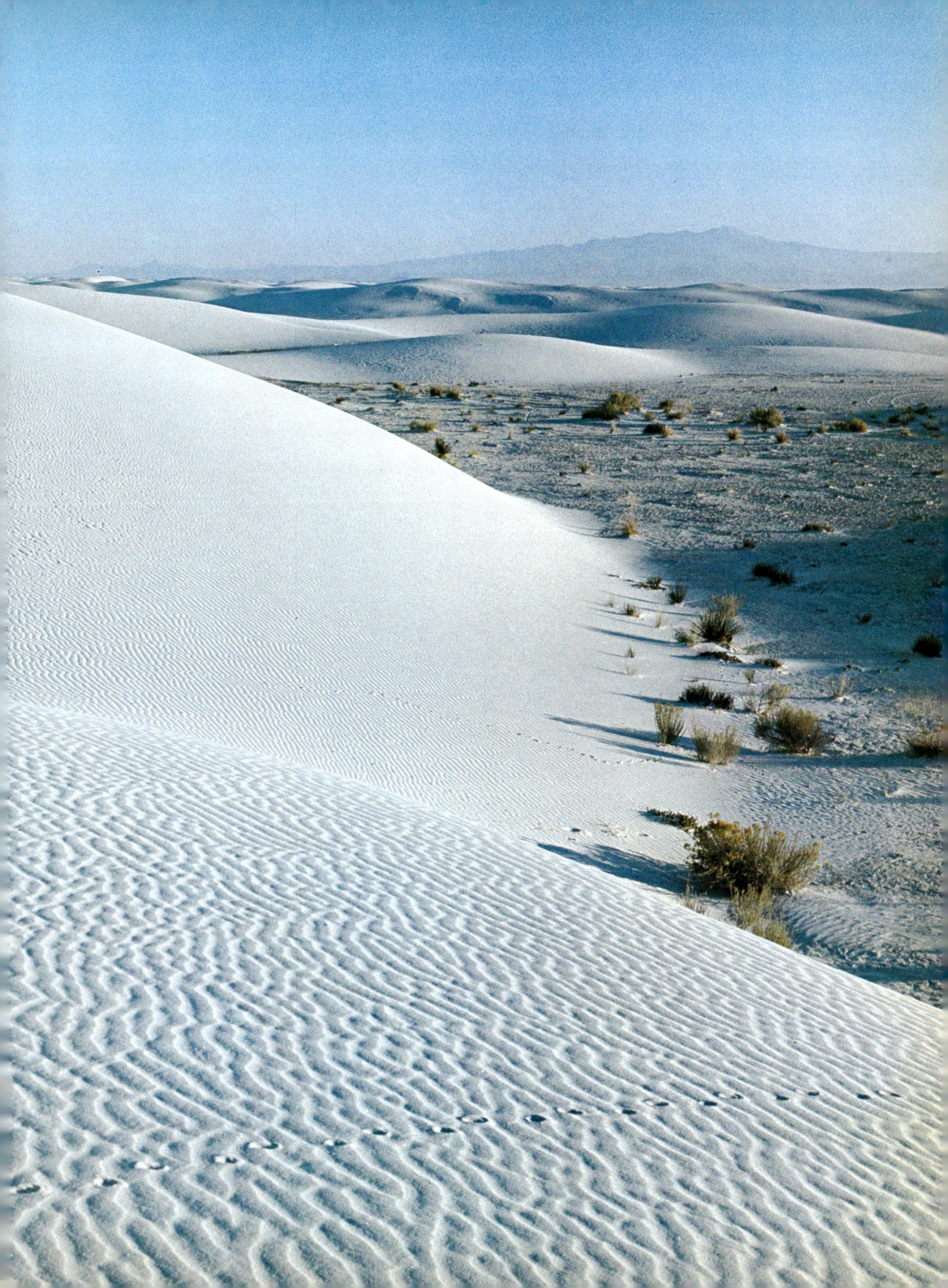

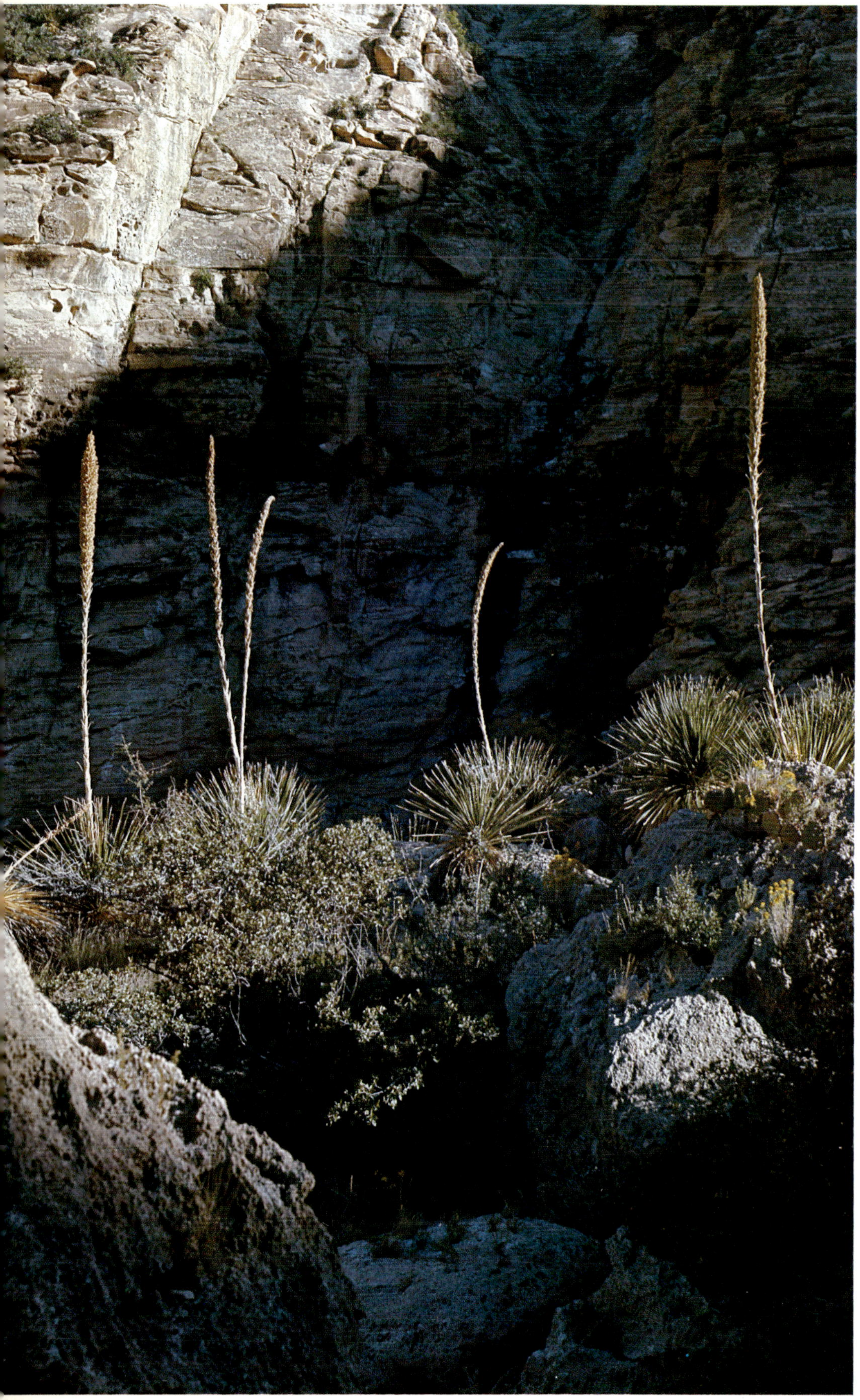

67

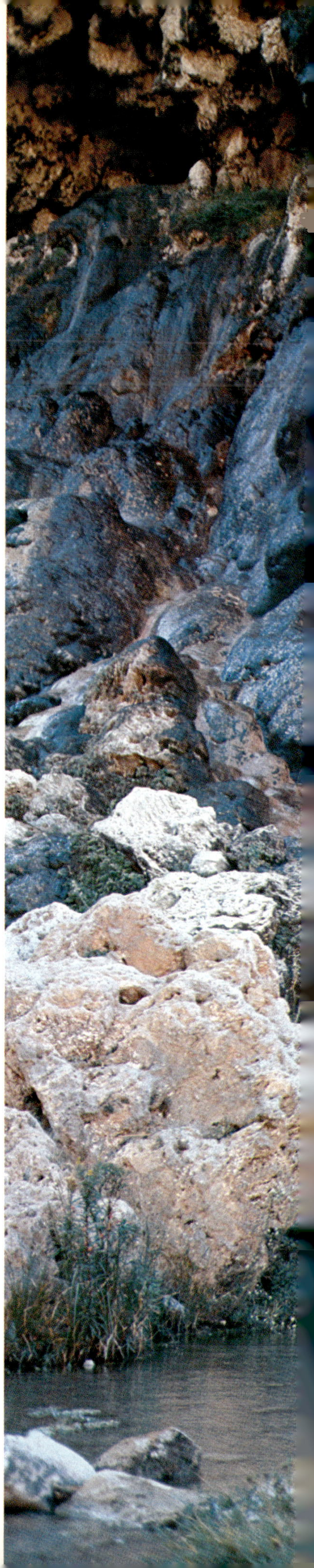

68

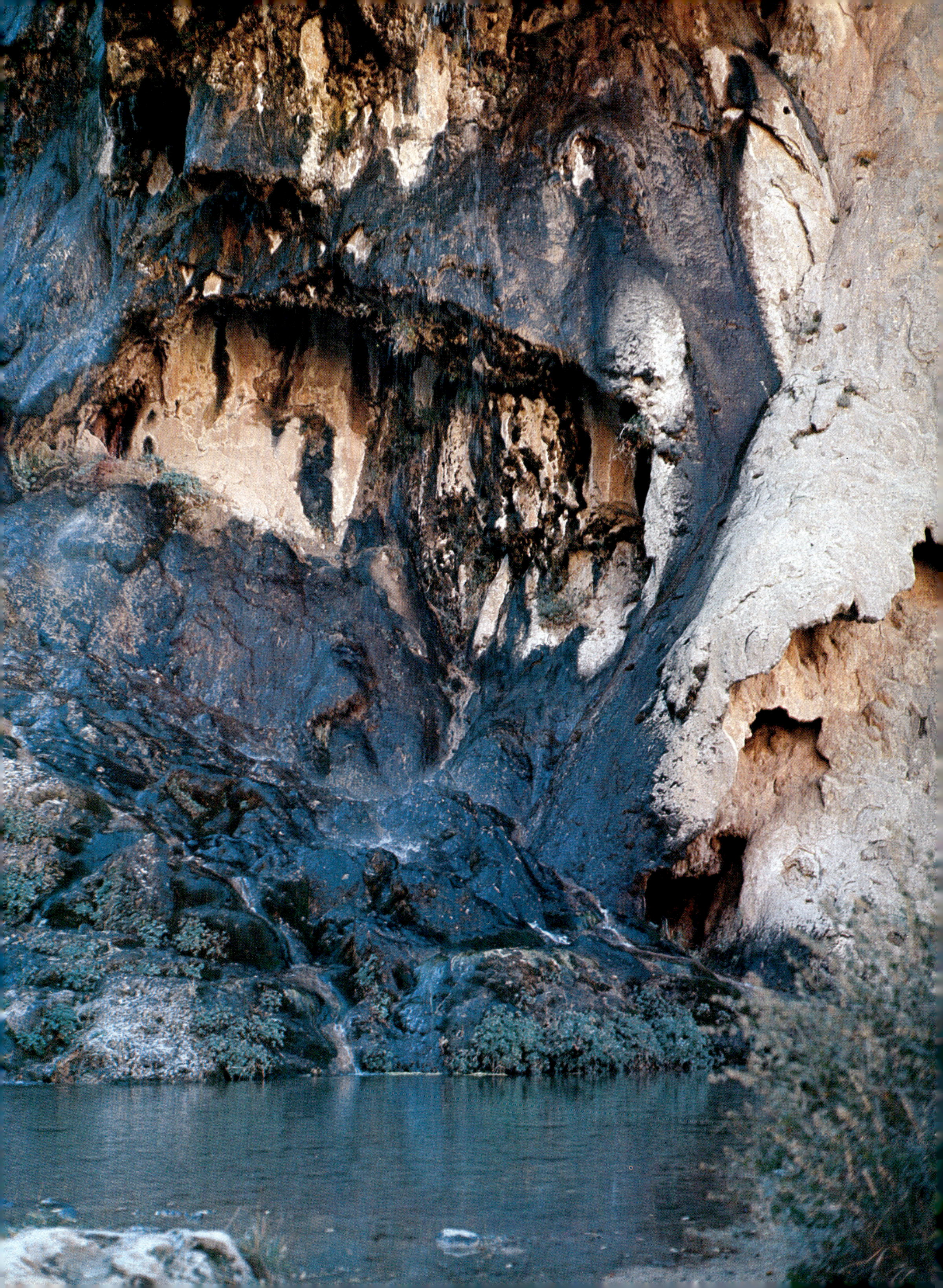

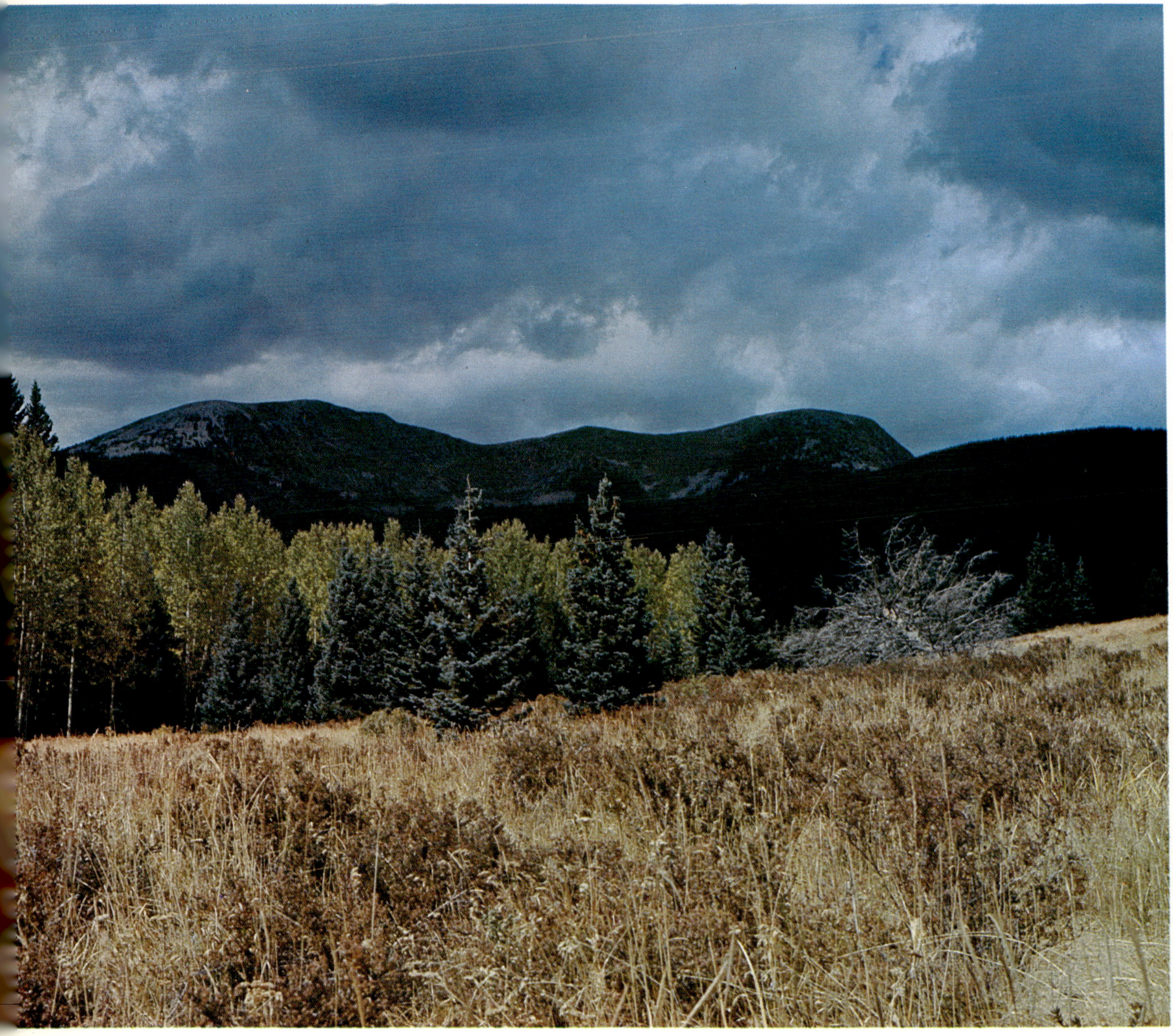

69

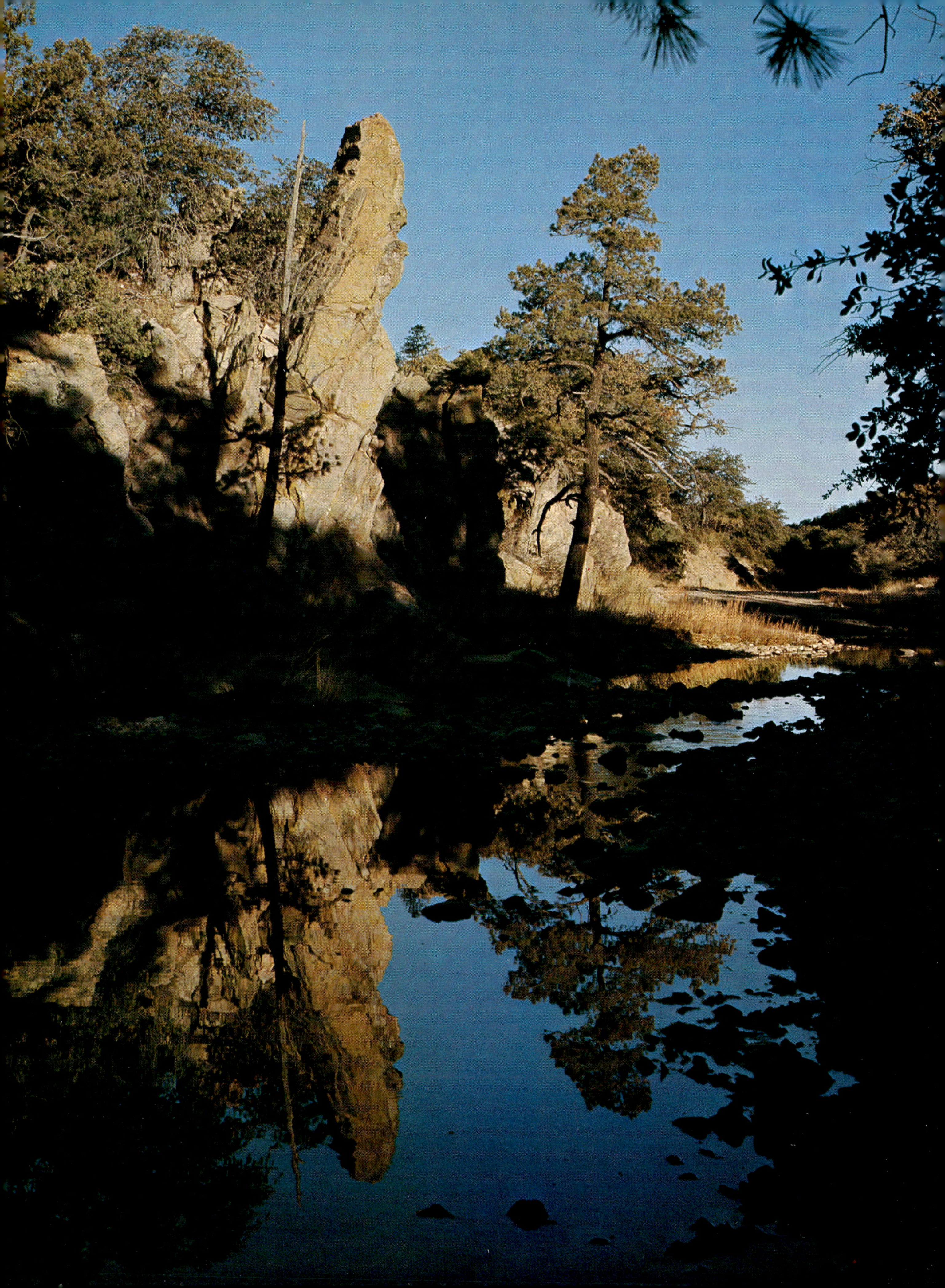

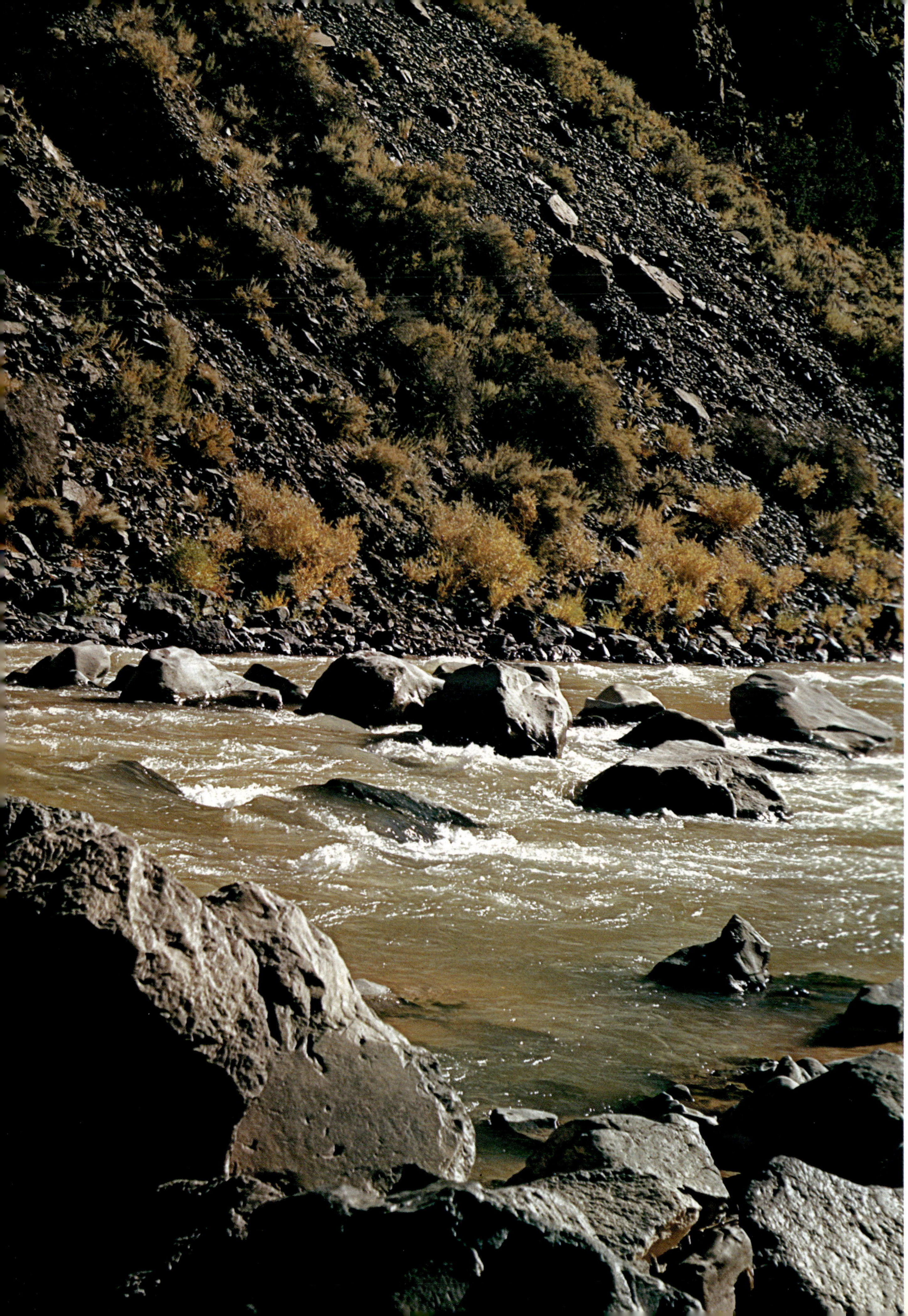

71

72

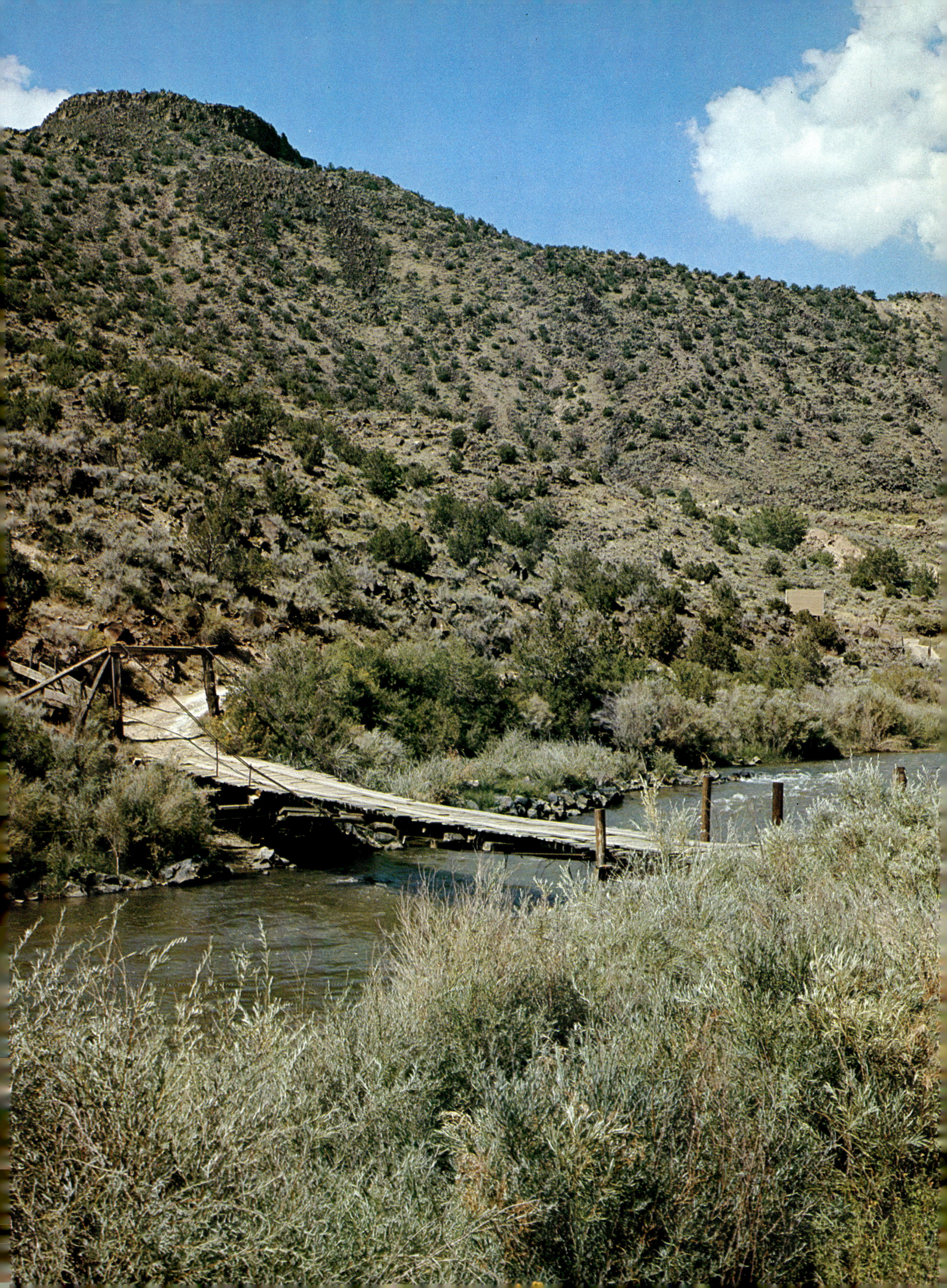

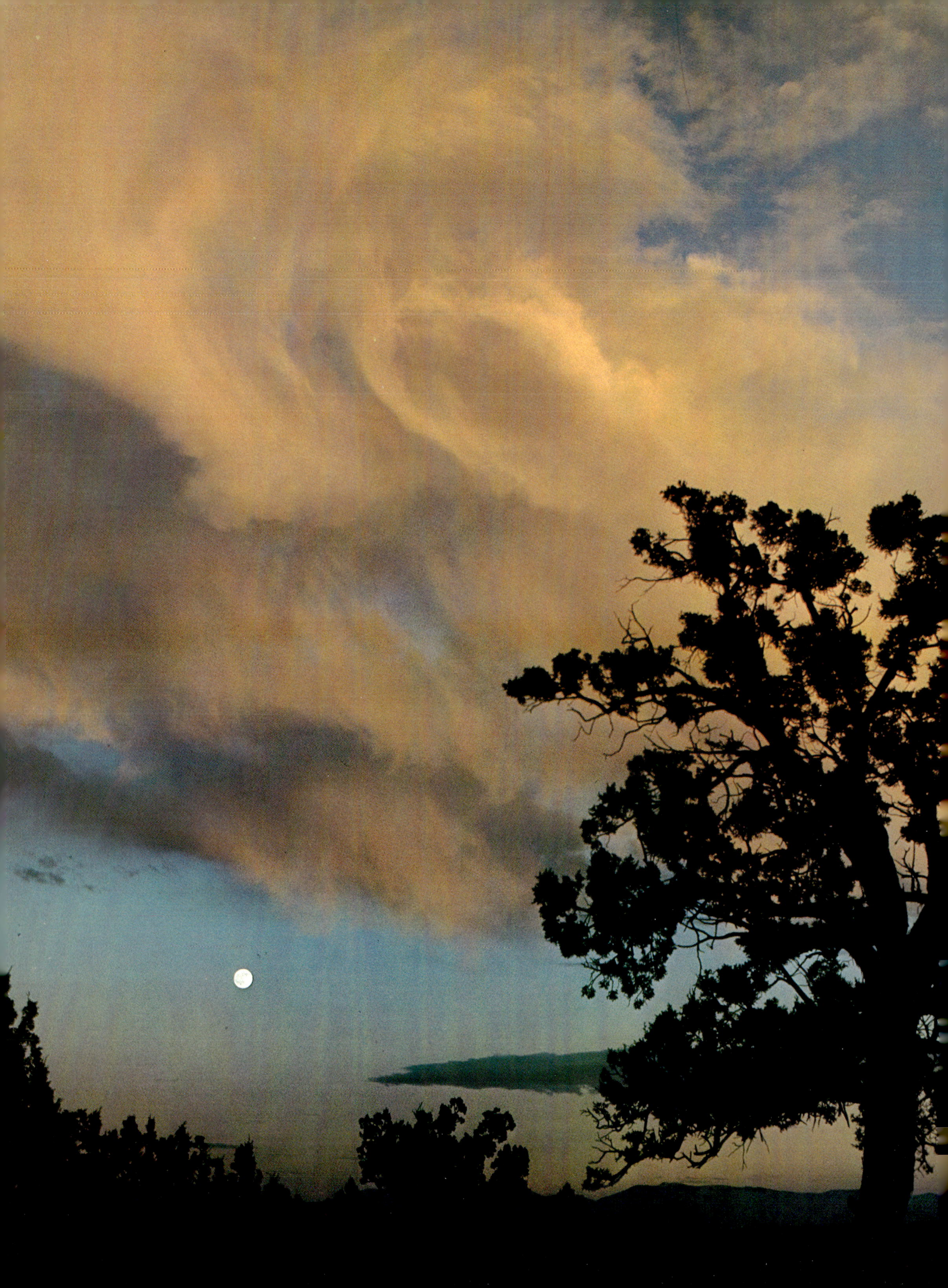

II

Looking to the Future

After these many centuries of human settlement New Mexico is still one of the least spoiled, most unusual places in the world. Many people come here to find a slower pace of life, to live more simply, and be inspired by the natural beauty and cultural variety. Yet, changes are affecting New Mexico that are inexorably bringing some of the problems that plague the quality of life elsewhere.

"IN CALIFORNIA, THEY INVENTED LOS ANGELES. IT DOESN'T WORK SO THEY ARE SENDING IT HERE." This was the headline of a full-page advertisement in one 1971 issue of the Albuquerque *Journal,* an attempt to alert the public to the dangers of a large-scale land speculation boom that is spreading across a million acres of New Mexico. The ad was paid for by the Central Clearing House in Santa Fe, one of the state's most active environmental organizations.

From Chama Valley to the pinyon- and juniper-covered hills around Santa Fe, from Cochiti to Deming, vast areas of wild land are being platted and scarred for new subdivisions—too often with little or no regard for, or understanding of, environmental consequences. There is not enough study of factors such as the availability of ground water, existing water rights, dangers of flash flooding and soil erosion, or the potential living conditions of the men, women, and children who may one day try to settle in these places.

By no means is this intended to suggest that all housing developments are environmentally abusive or ill-planned. But there is no doubt that New Mexico is extremely vulnerable to large-scale speculative land developments (some promoted by large out-of-state corporations) of the kind that have created outrageous conservation and consumer difficulties in such other states as Arizona, California, and Florida.

As Governor Bruce King of New Mexico, then a gubernatorial candidate, warned in 1970:

> We see growing up around us a number of real estate developments. These often involve a substantial change in the character of land use, as grazing, farming, and forest land is subdivided into homesites. In some cases of such development, the environmental effect of changing the land is ignored. . . . We can no longer afford the luxury of developers who care greatly for the monetary rewards involved in land-use, but who care little for the land itself.

Regarding the use of the state's limited water resources, there is a large loophole in New Mexico law which corporate land developers can and often do exploit, to the detriment of already existing water rights. This loophole permits an individual to drill a well to furnish water for a home, without requiring a public hearing and review by the State Engineer to determine whether, in fact, there is sufficient water available and whether existing rights will be infringed. Once the prospective home builder has made his application, the state simply issues a permit. Multiply the one home by hundreds or even thousands in a given area, and the result is a substantial drain on the water supply.

Obviously the law never anticipated the large-scale subdivisions now taking advantage of this provision. Consequently water that is already appropriated for other domestic, commercial, or agricultural uses is being, or eventually may be, depleted by extensive new housing developments. Ultimately there may not be enough water to go around. H. R. Stuckey, director of the U.S. Department of the Interior's New Mexico Office of Water Resources Research, has said: "The majority of land irrigated from groundwater draws its supply from non-recharging basins. Some areas have now completely exhausted the storage, and up to 200,000 acres are moving toward that point at an accelerating rate." A spokesman for the Central Clearing House, projecting the situation into the future, has concluded: "Looking at the amounts of groundwater in the state, we may be hard pressed to maintain our present uses within our children's lifetimes."

There is an old Indian proverb which says: "The frog does not drink up the pond in which he lives."

Air pollution—especially that from coal-burning power plants—is another serious threat to the environmental quality of New Mexico. In the Four Corners area of the Navajo Reservation, several coal-fired power plants have already been built, the largest of which is a few miles from Farmington. Describing this plant in his column in *The New York Times* (February 29, 1972), Tom Wicker said that it "is considered the worst air polluter in the United States, fouling the desert air over 10,000 miles from Albuquerque far into Arizona and Colorado." This single plant pollutes the air with three hundred fifty tons of fly ash and soot each day—more than is emitted by all sources in Los Angeles and New York City combined! In addition there are tremendous quantities of harmful sulfur dioxides and nitrogen oxides spewed into the air.

Pollution-abatement equipment, now required by New Mexico state law, may succeed in improving the situation somewhat, when and if the facilities are properly installed and maintained. But as other projected power plants are built in the region, including one that will apparently be the nation's largest, the once clear, healthful air of New Mexico may someday be among the most-polluted in the country.

To make matters worse, plans are now being implemented to begin converting high-sulfur coal to low-BTU gas at a number of locations in the United States. A pilot operation is planned soon for northwest New Mexico, to be followed by three full-scale plants. The application of this process has been delayed for many years, simply because the resulting air pollution is so severe. As Wicker pointed out: "These installations will wreak environmental havoc on an almost unimaginable scale. All will be fired by coal strip-mined in the area, a disaster in itself."

Strip mining the surface of the land for coal has, for years, been ravaging the Appalachia region of Kentucky, West Virginia, Ohio, and Pennsylvania. More recently stripping has begun in North Dakota, Montana, and Wyoming, and now New Mexico also is faced with the effects of these monstrous land-gouging operations, which—unless restored—leave vast corrugated landscapes of spoil bank windrows. Among current activities are a mine near Raton which supplies coal to a steel mill in California; a mine for the Public Service Company of New Mexico's San Juan Power Plant near Farmington; and Navajo Mine—the largest coal strip mine in the country—which supplies coal to Arizona Public Service Company's huge Four Corners Power Plant, also near Farmington. Navajo Mine is already stripping the land at about four hundred acres annually, and by 1985 it is expected to increase to more than a thousand acres.

The New Mexico Coal Surfacemining Commission, strongly backed by such public interest groups as the Rio Grande Chapter of the Sierra Club and Friends of the Earth, has so far proved determined to try to force the strip miners to agree to land restoration and revegetation programs. How well these agreements are actually enforced remains to be seen. According to the National Academy of Sciences, the arid Four Corners region is particularly difficult, if not impossible, to reclaim. And a 1972 U.S. Interior Department report pointed out that revegetation efforts there have thus far proved "minimal and unsuccessful."

A *New York Times* editorial of August 29, 1971, warned of the dangers of uncontrolled strip mining: "A *Times* survey indicates unmistakably that, unless a dangerous course is arrested, the shabby desolation of strip-mined regions in Appalachia will be reproduced on a monumentally larger scale from New Mexico to the State of Washington."

Copper smelters also pose an environmental and public health threat. New Mexico's largest is located near Silver City, spreading pollutants over a wide area. Other smelters lie upwind in southern Arizona. The U.S. Forest Service recently reported that copper smelter pollution is apparently damaging trees in some of the forested mountains, including the Gila National Forest. Research has revealed that needle tissue death is attributed to "acute sulfur dioxide injury." Medical tests of people living in the Silver City area are also revealing signs of severe health problems.

Meaningful pollution abatement facilities to protect the public health and welfare are of course very expensive. But their cost is, in the long run, far less than the harm inflicted upon human and environmental health, and should be either a necessary part of doing business or underwritten by government and thus by all taxpayers as part of the cost of running a highly industrialized civilization.

Another environmental problem is the controversial, government-sponsored tree-clearing program along some Southwestern rivers, which is strongly opposed by such groups as the National Audubon Society. A newspaper report of April 4, 1974, quotes the Society's view: "There has been no conclusive study or even tangible evidence that removing the trees and plants increases the flow of water in the river. On the contrary, the tight web of the root matrices of these plants hold in place the porous gravels and rocks. . . . The moisture-bearing leaves maintain a higher relative humidity over the water surface than is usual in areas where there are no trees, thus reducing evaporation. The plants act as windbreaks along the river banks, cutting down the force of hot, dry winds which also cause high evaporation. And, of course, the trees and underbrush offer valuable cover for wildlife." But the destruction of the great cottonwoods and other vegetation unfortunately continues along the Rio Grande and elsewhere.

Finally there is the problem of trying to protect the thousands of prehistoric Indian ruins that lie scattered about the land—most of them outside the boundaries of the few state and national monuments. For many years archaeologists have tried to salvage what artifacts and information they could, by keeping just ahead of pipeline company bulldozers. But now the new and less costly method of "preventative archaeology" is being applied as archaeologists accompany pipeline surveyors to help lay out routes that will avoid as many prehistoric sites as possible. Curtis Schaafsma, a field archaeologist working in the Southwest, is a pioneer of this important and promising new field.

The great challenge for New Mexicans in the future is to continue striving to live in harmony with the environment, as they have mostly succeeded in doing for centuries. As the Sierra Club's slogan so aptly puts it, the need is for: "Not blind opposition to progress, but opposition to blind progress." That, in the end, is what will keep New Mexico the unique and beautiful land it is today.

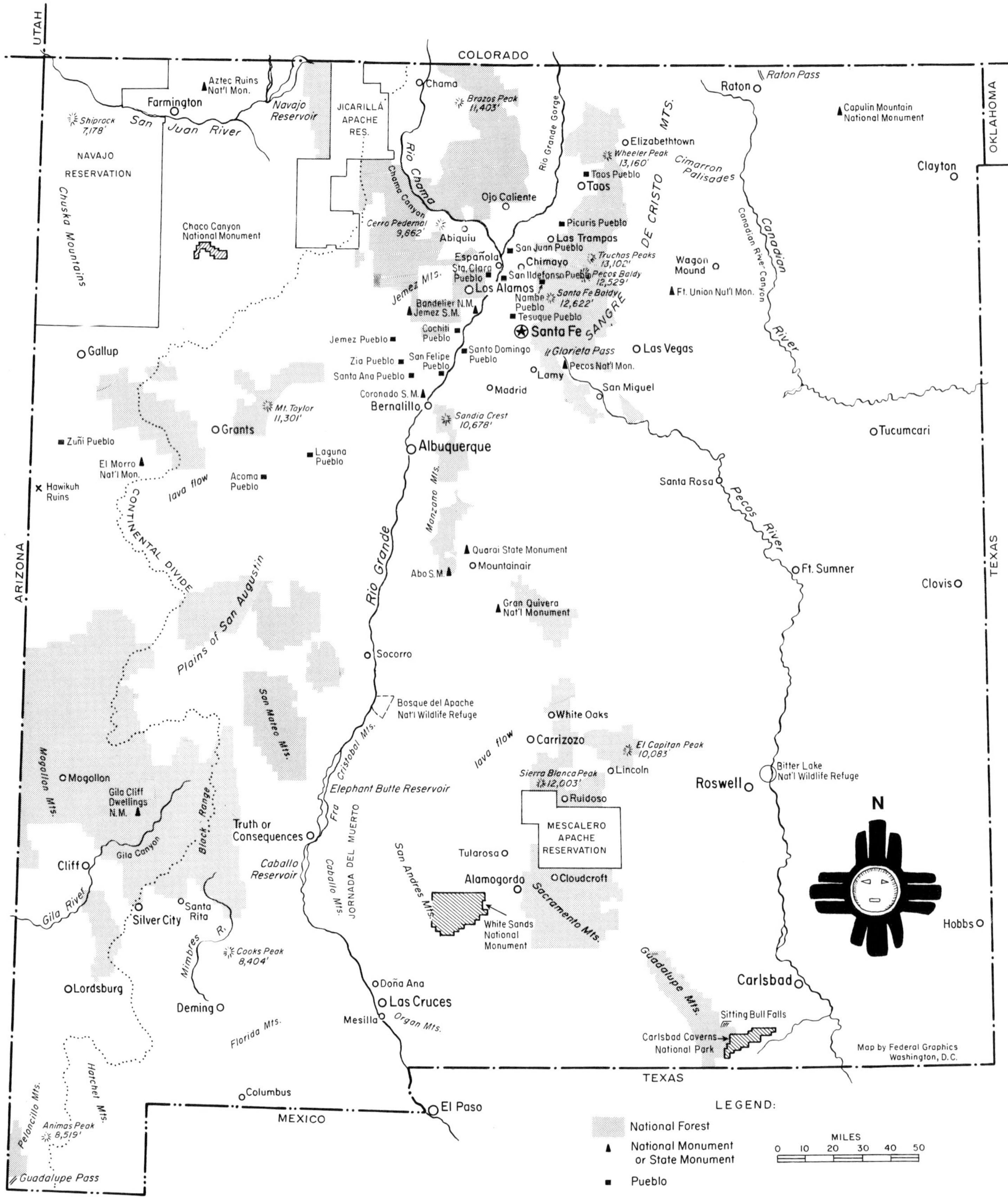
UTAH
COLORADO
OKLAHOMA
ARIZONA
TEXAS
TEXAS
MEXICO
Aztec Ruins Nat'l Mon.
Farmington
Shiprock 7,178'
San Juan River
Navajo Reservoir
NAVAJO RESERVATION
Chuska Mountains
Chaco Canyon National Monument
JICARILLA APACHE RES.
Chama
Brazos Peak 11,403'
Rio Chama
Chama Canyon
Rio Grande Gorge
Cerro Pedernal 9,862'
Abiquiu
Ojo Caliente
Raton
Raton Pass
Capulin Mountain National Monument
Elizabethtown
Wheeler Peak 13,160'
SANGRE DE CRISTO MTS.
Cimarron Palisades
Taos Pueblo
Taos
Clayton
Picuris Pueblo
Las Trampas
San Juan Pueblo
Truchas Peaks 13,102'
Española
Sta. Clara Pueblo
Chimayo
San Ildefonso Pueblo
Pecos Baldy 12,529'
Wagon Mound
Canadian River
Canadian River Canyon
Jemez Mts.
Los Alamos
Nambe Pueblo
Santa Fe Baldy 12,622'
Ft. Union Nat'l Mon.
Bandelier N.M.
Jemez S.M.
Tesuque Pueblo
Cochiti Pueblo
Santa Fe
Jemez Pueblo
Santo Domingo Pueblo
Glorieta Pass
Las Vegas
Gallup
Zia Pueblo
San Felipe Pueblo
Pecos Nat'l Mon.
Santa Ana Pueblo
Lamy
San Miguel
Madrid
Coronado S.M.
Mt. Taylor 11,301'
Bernalillo
Sandia Crest 10,678'
Grants
Tucumcari
Zuñi Pueblo
Laguna Pueblo
Albuquerque
El Morro Nat'l Mon.
Acoma Pueblo
Hawikuh Ruins
lava flow
Manzano Mts.
Santa Rosa
Pecos River
CONTINENTAL DIVIDE
Rio Grande
Quarai State Monument
Mountainair
Abo S.M.
Ft. Sumner
Clovis
Plains of San Augustin
Gran Quivera Nat'l Monument
Socorro
San Mateo Mts.
Bosque del Apache Nat'l Wildlife Refuge
White Oaks
Fra Cristobal Mts.
lava flow
Carrizozo
El Capitan Peak 10,083'
Mogollon Mts.
Mogollon
Sierra Blanca Peak 12,003'
Lincoln
Bitter Lake Nat'l Wildlife Refuge
Roswell
Elephant Butte Reservoir
Gila Cliff Dwellings N.M.
Ruidoso
Black Range
Truth or Consequences
JORNADA DEL MUERTO
MESCALERO APACHE RESERVATION
N
Gila Canyon
San Andres Mts.
Tularosa
Cliff
Caballo Reservoir
Caballo Mts.
Cloudcroft
Alamogordo
Sacramento Mts.
Gila River
Silver City
Santa Rita
White Sands National Monument
Hobbs
Mimbres R.
Cooks Peak 8,404'
Guadalupe Mts.
Lordsburg
Doña Ana
Carlsbad
Deming
Las Cruces
Mesilla
Organ Mts.
Sitting Bull Falls
Florida Mts.
Carlsbad Caverns National Park
Map by Federal Graphics Washington, D.C.
Hatchet Mts.
Columbus
Peloncillo Mts.
El Paso
LEGEND:
Animas Peak 8,519'
National Forest
National Monument or State Monument
Pueblo
MILES
0 10 20 30 40 50
Guadalupe Pass

Notes to the Plates

1 The Palisades, Cimarron Canyon

2 Casa Rinconada Kiva, Chaco Canyon National Monument

3 Wall detail, Chettro Kettle Ruin, Chaco Canyon

4 Pueblo Bonito at sunset

5, 6 Aztec Ruins National Monument

7, 8, 9 A pine grove, the Visitor Center, and a kiva in Ceremonial Cave, Bandelier National Monument

10 Tyuonyi Ruin, Bandelier National Monument

11, 12, 13 Snow scenes in the Jemez Mountains

14 Spanish village of Valdez below the Sangre de Cristo Mountains

15 Abandoned buildings in the old gold-mining town of Mogollon

16 Ruins of the Mutz Hotel in deserted Elizabethtown

17 Santa Fe Railway crossing near Roswell

18, 19, 20, 21 Views of the patio and church of the Monastery of Christ in the Desert, Chama Canyon

22 Irrigation ditch

23 Ranch at Mule Creek near the Arizona border

24 Cattleman

25 Branding irons

26 Cattle at a stock pond in San Simon Valley

27 Sunrise, Acoma Pueblo

28 Church of San Estevan, Acoma Pueblo

29 Dwellings in Acoma Pueblo

30 Petroglyph, Three Rivers, near Tularosa

31 Prehistoric Indian petroglyphs of mountain sheep and a Spanish inscription which says: "We pass by here, the Sergeant-Major and the Captain Juan de Archuleta and the Adjutant Diego Martin Barba and the Ensign Agustin de Ynojos, the year of 1636." El Morro National Monument

32 Inscription Rock, El Morro National Monument

33 Gate and wall, Canyon Road, Santa Fe

34 Chapel of San Miguel, Santa Fe

35 Sena Plaza, Santa Fe

36 Patio of Sena Plaza

37 Cathedral of Saint Francis, Santa Fe

38, 39 Mission La Purísima Concepción, Quarai State Monument, near Mountainair

40 Bennett Peak, a volcanic plug on the Navajo Reservation

41 Navajo weaver in the Chuska Mountains

42 Snakeweed

43 Sagebrush

44 Sunflowers

45 Corn fields along the San Juan River

46 Aspens and a distant rain storm, Pecos Wilderness Area

47 View into Wheeler Peak Wilderness from Taos Ski Valley

48, 49 Views in Gila Cliff Dwellings National Monument

50 Gila River Canyon in the Mogollon Mountains

51 Near the Gila River in the Mogollon Mountains

52 Zuñi, Acoma, and Zía Pueblo Indian storage jars from the Museum of New Mexico Collection

53 Rock formations near Zuñi

54 Skyrocket gilia

55 Canada wild rye

56 Autumn asters

57 Squirreltail grass

58 Indian paintbrush

59 Prickly pear cactus in full bloom

60 Red rock formation near Jemez Pueblo

61 Carlsbad Caverns (photograph by Devereux Butcher)

62 Slaughter Canyon in the Carlsbad Caverns National Park

63 Fruit-laden yucca

64 Prickly pear on the Malpais lava flow near Carrizozo

65 Cactus and ocotillo growing in Last Chance Canyon in the Guadalupe Mountains

66 Early morning, White Sands National Monument

67 Sotols growing in Sitting Bull Canyon

68 Pool at the foot of Sitting Bull Falls, Lincoln National Forest, in the Guadalupe Mountains

69 Pecos Baldy Peak in the Pecos Wilderness Area

70 Reflections in a stream, Peloncillo Mountains

71, 72 Scenes along the Rio Grande

73 Sunset and a juniper, Pajarito Plateau

Notes to the Drawings

Page

- 14 Prehistoric Mimbres beetle
- 17 Fish from a prehistoric Mimbres bowl
- 20 Moth motif from a Zuñi Pueblo jar
- 24 Bird and snake confrontation. Tesuque Pueblo
- 25 Parrot, typical motif of Acoma Pueblo
- 26 Highly stylized Zuñi "rain bird" motif
- 27 Prehistoric Mimbres fish
- 29 Double-necked marriage jar, typical of Santa Clara Pueblo's black polished ware
- 31 Double-headed bird of Acoma Pueblo
- 32 A black-on-black jar with plumed serpent motif by María and Julian Martinez of San Ildefonso Pueblo
- 35 Stylized bird of San Ildefonso Pueblo
- 36 Cochiti Pueblo bird, possibly a roadrunner
- 38 Prehistoric Mimbres grasshopper
- 42 Wild turkey from a Mimbres bowl
- 43 Bat from a Zía Pueblo jar
- 45 Rare bird-and-flower motif from Santo Domingo Pueblo
- 46 Typical Zuñi storage jar, with design of deer, birds, and flower rosettes
- 47 Typical Santo Domingo jar with bold, simple geometric designs (Collection Denver Art Museum)
- 48 Prehistoric Mimbres motif of a whip scorpion or vinegarroon, so named for its ability to spray strong-smelling acetic acid
- 48 Zía Pueblo sun symbol from which New Mexico's official emblem was taken
- 123 Drawing by the author of a *bulto* of Saint John the Baptist made by Ben Ortega

Chronology

15,000 plus years ago	Sandia man, hunters of mastodon and mammoth, live in the high plains and mountains of New Mexico.
11,000 to 12,000 years ago	Folsom man, hunters of great bison, range the plains.
700 to 900 years ago	Climax of the Anasazi pueblos at Chaco Canyon.
500 to 700 years ago	Pueblo Indians inhabit Pajarito Plateau.
400 to 700 years ago	Pueblo Indians settle along the Rio Grande.
1540 to 1542	Coronado leads the first Spanish exploration into New Mexico.
1598	First successful colonization, by Oñate.
1610	Santa Fe founded.
1620s to 1630s	Many Franciscan missions founded at pueblos.
1680	Pueblo rebellion overthrows Spanish rule.
1692	Spaniards under de Vargas reconquer New Mexico.
1706	Albuquerque founded.
1750s	Mountain villages of Las Trampas and Truchas founded.
1803	United States buys Louisiana Territory from France.
1807	U.S. Lieutenant Zebulon M. Pike tours New Mexico under Spanish military escort.
1821	Mexico declares independence from Spain. William Becknell founds the Santa Fe Trail.
1824	Becknell leads first wagon train across the Great Plains.

1820s	Beaver trapping booms in the Rocky Mountain West. Taos is an important base and resort.
1841	A group of Texans tries unsuccessfully to take over New Mexico.
1845	President James K. Polk declares war on Mexico.
1846	Mexican General Armijo surrenders New Mexico to U.S. General Kearny without firing a shot.
1847	New Mexico Governor Charles Bent killed in Taos Pueblo uprising instigated by an embittered ex-Mexican colonel.
1848	Treaty of Guadalupe. Mexico formally gives up all claims to New Mexico, California, and Texas.
1850	New Mexico becomes a U.S. territory.
1853	Gadsden Purchase; U.S. acquires southern part of New Mexico from Mexico.
1858 to 1859	St. Louis-to-San Francisco Butterfield Stage Line runs via Mesilla and southern New Mexico.
1861 to 1862	Confederate soldiers take and hold Albuquerque and Santa Fe until defeated by Fort Union troops and Colorado volunteers.
1863	Congress carves off western half of New Mexico to establish the Territory of Arizona.
1864 to 1868	Navajos held captive at Bosque Redondo Reservation.
1864	Beginning of eastern New Mexico cattle drives along the Goodnight-Loving Trail.
1869 to 1886	Archbishop Jean Baptiste Lamy directs construction of French Romanesque Saint Francis Cathedral in Santa Fe.
1878	Santa Fe Railway reaches New Mexico via Raton Pass.
1870s	Lieutenant George M. Wheeler leads scientific survey of 57 million acres of New Mexico and the Southwest.

1886	Drought and blizzards wipe out huge cattle boom on Great Plains.
	Apache chief Geronimo finally surrenders in Peloncillo Mountains.
1860s to 1890s	Mining booms throughout New Mexico.
1891	Beginning of national forest reserves in New Mexico.
1909	Museum of New Mexico founded.
1912	New Mexico becomes a state.
1924	Gila Wilderness established—first wilderness area in America.

Some Further Reading

Arnberger, Leslie. *Flowers of the Southwest Mountains.* Globe, Arizona: Southwest Parks & Monuments Association, 1952, 1974.
Bahti, Tom. *Southwestern Indian Ceremonials.* Las Vegas, Nevada: KC Publications, 1971.
———. *Southwestern Indian Tribes.* Las Vegas, Nevada: KC Publications, 1968.
Bandelier, Adolf F. *The Delight Makers.* New York: Dodd, Mead & Co., 1890.
Bradford, Richard. *Red Sky at Morning.* Philadelphia: Lippincott, 1968.
Bullock, Alice. *Mountain Villages.* Santa Fe: The Sunstone Press, 1973.
Cather, Willa. *Death Comes for the Archbishop.* New York: Alfred A. Knopf, Inc., 1926.
Chavez, Fray Angelico. *My Penitent Land.* Albuquerque: University of New Mexico Press, 1974.
Church, Peggy Pond. *The House at Otowi Bridge.* Albuquerque: University of New Mexico Press, 1959.
Corbett, John M. *Aztec Ruins National Monument.* Washington, D.C.: U.S. Government Printing Office, 1962.
Dickey, Roland F. *New Mexico Village Arts.* Albuquerque: University of New Mexico Press, 1952, 1973.
Dodge, Natt N. *Flowers of the Southwest Deserts.* Globe, Arizona: Southwest Parks & Monuments Association, 1951, 1973.
———. *The Natural History Story of White Sands National Monument.* Globe, Arizona: Southwest Parks & Monuments Association, 1971.
Dozier, Edward P. *The Pueblo Indians of North America.* New York: Holt, Rinehart & Winston, Inc., 1970.
Dunn, Dorothy. *American Indian Painting.* Albuquerque: University of New Mexico Press, 1968.
Dutton, Bertha P. *Friendly People: The Zuñi Indians.* Santa Fe: Museum of New Mexico Press, 1963, 1968.
———. *Navaho Weaving Today.* Santa Fe: Museum of New Mexico Press, 1961, 1968.
———. *Sun Father's Way: The Kiva Murals of Kuaua.* Albuquerque: University of New Mexico Press, 1963.
Fergusson, Erna. *Dancing Gods.* Albuquerque: University of New Mexico Press, 1931.
Gilpin, Laura. *The Enduring Navaho.* Austin: University of Texas Press, 1968.

Gonzáles, Clara. *The Shalakos Are Coming.* Santa Fe: Museum of New Mexico Press, 1966, 1969.

Gonzáles, Nancie L. *The Spanish-Americans of New Mexico: A Heritage of Pride.* Albuquerque: University of New Mexico Press, 1967.

Hannum, Alberta. *Paint the Wind.* New York: The Viking Press, Inc., 1958; Ballantine Books, 1972.

———. *Spin a Silver Dollar.* New York: The Viking Press, Inc., 1944, 1970; Ballantine Books, 1972.

Harlow, Francis H., and John V. Young. *Contemporary Pueblo Indian Pottery.* Santa Fe: Museum of New Mexico Press, 1965.

Hayes, Alden C. *The Four Churches of Pecos.* Albuquerque: University of New Mexico Press, 1974.

Historic Santa Fe Foundation, The. *Old Santa Fe Today.* Albuquerque: University of New Mexico Press, 1966, 1972.

Horgan, Paul. *Great River: The Rio Grande in North American History,* 2 vols. New York: Holt, Rinehart & Winston, 1954; Pleasantville, New York: Minerva Press, Reader's Digest Books, Inc., 1968.

———. *The Centuries of Santa Fe.* New York: E. P. Dutton & Co., Inc., 1956.

Hyde, Philip. *Navajo Wildlands.* San Francisco: Sierra Club, 1967; New York: Ballantine Books–Sierra Club, 1969.

Jenkinson, Michael, and Karl Kernberger. *Ghost Towns of New Mexico: Playthings of the Wind.* Albuquerque: University of New Mexico Press, 1967.

Kidder, Alfred V. *An Introduction to the Study of Southwestern Archaeology.* New Haven: Yale University Press, 1924, 1973.

Kluckhohn, Clyde, and Dorothea Leighton. *The Navaho.* Cambridge: Harvard University Press, 1946, 1958; Garden City, New York: Natural History Library, 1962.

LaFarge, Oliver. *Laughing Boy.* Boston: Houghton Mifflin Co., 1929, 1957.

Ligon, J. Stokley. *New Mexico Birds and Where to Find Them.* Albuquerque: University of New Mexico Press, 1961.

Lummis, Charles F. *The Land of Poco Tiempo.* New York: Charles Scribner's Sons, 1893; Albuquerque: University of New Mexico Press, 1973.

McFarland, Elizabeth F. *Forever Frontier: The Gila Cliff Dwellings.* Albuquerque: University of New Mexico Press, 1967, 1972.

Marriott, Alice. *María: The Potter of San Ildefonso.* Norman: University of Oklahoma Press, 1948, 1970.

Olin, George. *Mammals of the Southwest Deserts.* Globe, Arizona: Southwest Parks & Monuments Association, 1954, 1970.

———. *Mammals of the Southwest Mountains and Mesas.* Globe, Arizona: Southwest Parks & Monuments Association, 1961, 1971.

Ortiz, Alfonso. *The Tewa World.* Chicago: The University of Chicago Press, 1969, 1971.

Patraw, Pauline M. *Flowers of the Southwest Mesas.* Globe, Arizona: Southwest Parks & Monuments Association, 1951, 1970.

Pearce, T. M. *New Mexico Place Names: A Geographical Dictionary.* Albuquerque: University of New Mexico Press, 1965.
Richter, Conrad. *The Sea of Grass.* New York: Alfred A. Knopf, Inc., 1937; Bantam Books, 1971.
Schaafsma, Polly. *Rock Art of New Mexico.* Santa Fe: State Planning Office, 1972.
Shishkin, J. K. *The Palace of the Governors.* Santa Fe: Museum of New Mexico Press, 1973.
Sonnichsen, C. L. *The Mescalero Apaches.* Norman: University of Oklahoma Press, 1958.
Thomas, Justine, and David King. *Santa Fe: The City Different.* Santa Fe: The Sunstone Press, 1973.
Thrapp, Dan L. *The Conquest of Apacheria.* Norman: University of Oklahoma Press, 1967.
Ungnade, Herbert E. *Guide to New Mexico Mountains.* Albuquerque: University of New Mexico Press, 1965, 1972.
Utley, Robert M. *Fort Union National Monument.* Washington, D.C.: U.S. Government Printing Office, 1962.
Waters, Frank. *Masked Gods.* Denver: Sage Books, 1950.
———. *The Man Who Killed the Deer.* New York: Farrar and Rinehart, 1942.
Wing, Kittredge A. *Bandelier National Monument.* Washington, D.C.: U.S. Government Printing Office, 1955, 1961.
Wormington, H. M. *Prehistoric Indians of the Southwest.* Denver: Denver Museum of Natural History, 1956, 1970.